Efficient Similarity Search Techniques for Textual and Non-Textual Datasets

By,
Sachendra Singh Chauhan

Efficient Similarity Search Techniques for Textual and Non-Textual Datasets

by
Sachendra Singh Chauhan

List of Abbreviations

COD	Curse of Dimensionality
BF	Bloom Filter
MBF	Matrix Bloom Filter
CBF	Counting Bloom Filter
IBF	Invertible Bloom Filter
ICBF	Invertible Counting Bloom Filter
SBT	Sequence Bloom Tree
AMQ	Approximate Membership Query
LSBF	Locality-Sensitive Bloom Filter
LSH	Locative-Sensitive Hashing
DSH	Density Sensitive Hashing
NN	Nearest Neighbor
ANN	Approximate Nearest Neighbor
PDS	Probabilistic Data Structure
TF-IDF	Term Frequency-Inverse Document Frequency
ADC	Automatic Document Classification
QBT	Query by Text
CBDR	Content Based Data Retrieval
CBIR	Content Based Image Retrieval
GPU	Graphics Processing Unit
CUDA	Compute Unified Device Architecture
SIMD	Single Instruction, Multiple Data
DCD	Dominant Color Descriptor
WATH	Weighted Average of Triangular Histogram
HSV	Hue Saturation Value
RGB	Red Green Blue
SIFT	Scale Invariant Feature Transform
LIOP	Local Intensity Order Pattern
BoVW	Bag of Visual Words

LBP	Binary Local Pattern
ZM	Zernike Moments
LDRP	Local Derivative Radial Pattern
SED	Structural Elements' Descriptor
MSD	Micro-structure Descriptor
PSO	Particle Swarm Optimization
PQ	Product Quantization
CNN	Convolutional Neural Network
MH	Min Hash
CM	Characteristic Matrix
SM	Signature Matrix

Abstract

In today's information overloaded world, data has become the epicentre of the entire research. Textual data in the form of log, news papers, web documents, *etc.* is a key source of data analytics. Apart from textual contents, images, videos, audios generated by various handy devices are shared and downloaded by millions of users across the globe, every second. Finding similar items in such large and unstructured datasets (text and image) is indeed a challenging task. The exact match rarely has meaning in these environments; proximity or distance among the items is a preferred choice to identify similar items.

In this work three similarity search approaches have been proposed: one for text documents and two for image datasets. For the textual data, a parallel similarity search approach has been proposed which uses Bloom filters for the representation of the features of the document and comparison with user's query. Query features are stored in an integer array. The proposed approach uses approximate similarity search; has been implemented on Graphics Processing Unit (GPU) with compute unified device architecture as the programming platform.

Two approaches have been proposed for image dataset. Both approaches uses Content Based Image Retrieval (CBIR). First CBIR approach named as 'Bi-layer Content Based Image Retrieval (BiCBIR) System' consists of two modules: first module extracts the features of images in terms of color, texture and shape. Second module consists of two layers: initially all images are compared with query image for shape and texture feature space and indexes of M images similar to the query image are retrieved. Next, M images retrieved from previous layer are matched with query image for shape and color feature space and finally F images similar to the query image are returned as output.

Second approach, Feature wise Incremental CBIR, named as FiCBIR, uses color, texture, and shape features. The retrieval process is accomplished in three layers, in the first layer complete dataset is searched but only one feature space is used. Top 10% of images most similar to query image are retained in the second layer. The second layer uses two features for similarity computation and only 50% of the most similar images are passed to the third layer. Finally, the third layer uses all three features to compute the similarity. It has been experimentally proved that FiCBIR reduces the search space at subsequent layers by using multiple features for a reduced dataset in the final layer.

The proposed CBIR approaches are evaluated on publicly available image datasets and experimental results validate the effectiveness of the approaches. The performance of both the approaches outperform the available state-of-the-art image retrieval systems in terms of precision, recall and f-score.

Contents

List of Figures		vi
List of Tables		viii
List of Algorithms		ix
List of Abbreviations		x
Certificate		xiii
Acknowledgements		xiii
Abstract		xiv

1 Introduction   **1**

   1.1 Distance Measure Functions 2
      1.1.1 Euclidean Distance 3
      1.1.2 Hamming Distance 3
      1.1.3 Edit Distance 4
      1.1.4 Jaccard Distance 4
      1.1.5 Dice Coefficient 4
      1.1.6 Cosine Distance 4
   1.2 Models of Similarity Search 5
      1.2.1 Vector Space Model 5
      1.2.2 Metric Space Model 5
            1.2.2.1 Non-Metric Space Model 6
   1.3 Probabilistic Data Structures for Similarity Search 6
      1.3.1 Bloom Filter 6
      1.3.2 Variants of Bloom Filter for Similarity Search 9

		1.3.2.1	Matrix Bloom Filter	9

                    1.3.2.2   Bloofi 9

                    1.3.2.3   Sequence Bloom Tree 10

          1.3.3   Min Hash 11

                    1.3.3.1   Steps in Min Hash 12

          1.3.4   Locality-Sensitive Hashing 12

    1.4   Similarity Search Approaches 14

          1.4.1   Partitioning 14

          1.4.2   Approximation 15

    1.5   Similarity Search using GPU 15

          1.5.1   GPU Computing 16

          1.5.2   Compute Unified Device Architecture (CUDA) 16

    1.6   Role of Similarity Search in Data Intensive Applications 17

          1.6.1   Document Clustering 17

          1.6.2   Plagiarism Detection 18

          1.6.3   Recommender System 18

          1.6.4   Health Care System 18

          1.6.5   Fingerprints Matching 19

          1.6.6   Face Recognition 19

    1.7   Thesis Organization 19

2 Literature Review   **21**

    2.1   Approximate Similarity Search 21

    2.2   Similarity Search through Parallel Processing 24

    2.3   Similarity Search in Text based Applications 26

          2.3.1   Text Features Extraction Techniques 27

                    2.3.1.1   Shingling 27

                    2.3.1.2   Bag of Words (BOW) 27

                    2.3.1.3   Content Defined Chucking (CDC) 27

          2.3.2   Summary of Text Retrieval Approaches 27

2.4	Similarity Search in Images		29
	2.4.1	Image Features Extraction	29
	2.4.2	Feature Merging	30
	2.4.3	Content Based Image Retrieval	31
	2.4.4	Summary of Image Retrieval Approaches	34
2.5	Problem Statement		38
2.6	Research Objectives		38

3 A Parallel Computational Approach for Similarity Search using Bloom Filters (PCASSB) — 39

3.1	Proposed approach			39
	3.1.1	Offline Module		41
		3.1.1.1	Preprocessing of Documents	41
		3.1.1.2	Creation of Bloom Filters from Shingle Sets	41
	3.1.2	Online Module		43
		3.1.2.1	Query Pre-processing	43
		3.1.2.2	Similarity Search	43
		3.1.2.3	Ranking	47
3.2	Experimental Results and Analysis			48
	3.2.1	Dataset		48
	3.2.2	Parameter Setting		48
	3.2.3	System Configuration		49
	3.2.4	Experimental Results		49
		3.2.4.1	Similarity Score of Documents Corresponding to Query	49
		3.2.4.2	Query Search Time in CPU and GPU	52

4 Similarity Search Approaches for Image Datasets — 56

4.1	Introduction		56
4.2	Image Feature Extraction		58
	4.2.1	Color Feature Extraction	58
	4.2.2	Texture Feature Extraction	59

		4.2.3	Shape Feature Extraction	60
	4.3	Similarity Computation		62
	4.4	An Efficient bi-layer CBIR approach (BiCBIR)		63
		4.4.1	Retrieval of Images Similar to the Query Image in BiCBIR	65
	4.5	Efficient layer-wise Feature incremental approach for CBIR system (FiCBIR)		67
		4.5.1	Retrieval of Images Similar to the Query Image in FiCBIR	67
5	**Implementation Details and Experimental Results**			**72**
	5.1	Implementation Details		72
		5.1.1	System Configuration	72
		5.1.2	Datasets	72
		5.1.3	Evaluation Parameters	73
	5.2	Experimental Results of BiCBIR		73
		5.2.1	Variants of CBIR	74
		5.2.2	Number of Processing Steps in BiCBIR	75
		5.2.3	Comparison of BiCBIR with Other Approaches	83
	5.3	Experimental Results of FiCBIR		90
		5.3.1	Number of Processing Steps and Retrieval Precision in FiCBIR	103
6	**Conclusion and Future Scope**			**107**
	6.1	Conclusion		107
	6.2	Contributions		108
	6.3	Future Scope		109
	References			**111**
	List of Publications			**130**

Chapter 1

Introduction

Similarity search is a process of retrieving similar items from the reference dataset in response to the user's query. Formally, similarity search can be defined as the process of retrieving k items, $I = (I_1, I_2, I_3, \ldots, I_k)$, which have similarity score higher than the remaining of the items or have similarity score S_c greater than the predefined threshold θ from the reference dataset R_D, corresponding to the user's query Q. Fig. 1.1 gives the diagrammatic representation of data in k-Nearest Neighbor with k similar items query. Here $I_1, I_2, I_3, \ldots$ represent the data items, q is query item, k is an integer number. The query q in case of k-NN retrieves the k most similar items. Fig. 1.2 shows similarity search in r-NN with r_1 and r_2 as two distance thresholds and all the items having similarity score greater than r_1 or r_2 are retrieved.

Similarity search has become a primary computational task in various application domains which including pattern recognition, data mining, biomedical databases, mul-

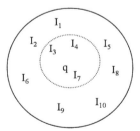

Figure 1.1: k-Nearest Neighbors

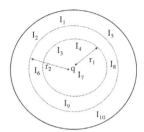

Figure 1.2: r-Nearest Neighbors

timedia information retrieval, machine learning, data compression, computer vision, statistical data analysis, *etc*. All these applications process large and high dimensional data. Too many dimensions cause every observation in the dataset to appear equidistant from each other. This high dimensionality of data creates problem for similarity search, commonly referred as curse of dimensionality (COD) [5]. To overcome the problems caused by COD, two approaches generally considered in similarity search are: approximate processing and parallel processing. Approximate processing reduces the search time by avoiding the exhaustive searching process whereas in parallel processing, similarity search time is reduced by using large number of processing units. By combining parallel and approximate processing, similarity search problems can be solved in less time and space.

Similarity search approaches for text or image datasets follow three major steps:

- Pre-processing and feature extraction of data under consideration.
- Similarity computation between features of query item and dataset.
- Ranking of retrieved objects based on similarity score.

An overview of content based text or image retrieval systems is depicted in Fig. 1.3.

1.1 Distance Measure Functions

Similarity computation between pair feature vectors is essential for retrieval of similar items corresponding to the query item. It is computed by using a suitable distance

Chapter 1 Introduction

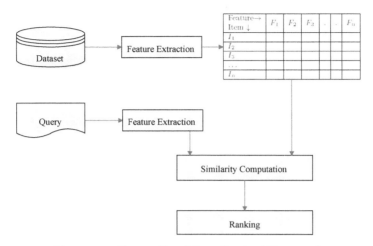

Figure 1.3: Content Based Data Retrieval Framework

measure function. The choice of similarity or distance measure function depends upon the type of data and application under consideration. Various similarity and distance measure functions are discussed in following subsections.

1.1.1 Euclidean Distance

Euclidean distance computes the distance between two objects A and B in Euclidean space. The Euclidean distance between two points is the length of the path connecting them.

$$Euclidean_{Distance} = \sqrt{\sum_{i=1}^{n}(A_i - B_i)^2} \qquad (1.1)$$

If the data under consideration is dense or continuous, this is the one of the most efficient distance measure functions.

1.1.2 Hamming Distance

The *hamming distance* between two boolean vectors of equal length is the number of positions at which these vectors vary. Formally, it is a count of the number of ones when XOR operation is applied on two boolean vectors.

1.1.3 Edit Distance

In general, *Edit distance* is used for measuring the similarity of the strings in vector space. For two strings $x = x_1, x_2, \ldots, x_n$ and $y = y_1, y_2, \ldots, y_m$, the minimum number of times the insertions and deletions of single characters done to convert x to y or y to x is the Edit distance between them.

1.1.4 Jaccard Distance

To calculate *Jaccard distance*, first the Jaccard similarity is calculated and then the Jaccard distance (Eq. 1.3). Jaccard similarity between two sets is defined as the cardinality of the common items of sets divided by the cardinality of the unique items of the sets (Eq. 1.2).

$$Jaccard_{Similarity} = \frac{A \cap B}{A \cup B} \qquad (1.2)$$

$$Jaccard_{Distance} = 1 - Jaccard_{Similarity} \qquad (1.3)$$

1.1.5 Dice Coefficient

Dice coefficient [6] is used for similarity computation of two sets. It is similar to Jaccard similarity but it uses sum of number of items in both sets instead of union. Dice coefficient (D_c) is given by:

$$D_c(set_1, set_2) = \frac{2 \times C_{ic}}{S_{ic}^1 + S_{ic}^2} \qquad (1.4)$$

where C_{ic} represents common items in set_1 and set_2; S_{ic}^1 and S_{ic}^2 represent total items in set_1 and set_2 respectively.

1.1.6 Cosine Distance

Cosine distance is a dual of cosine similarity. To calculate the cosine distance (Eq. 1.6), first cosine similarity is calculated. Cosine similarity is a proximity measure which calculates the normalized dot product of the two points (Eq. 1.5). If the cosine is 0°, *i.e.*, angle between two point is 1, items are similar. If two points are at 90°, there similarity score is 0. This measure is quite efficient in evaluating sparse vectors.

$$Cosine_{Similarity} = \frac{\sum\limits_{i=1}^{n} A_i B_i}{\sqrt{\sum\limits_{i=1}^{n} A_i^2} \sqrt{\sum\limits_{i=1}^{n} B_i^2}} \tag{1.5}$$

$$Cosine_{Distance} = 1 - Cosine_{Similarity} \tag{1.6}$$

1.2 Models of Similarity Search

1.2.1 Vector Space Model

Vector space model is an algebraic model used for representing the text files and query in vector form where elements of the vectors are shingles or bag of words that represent the features of the text files. Success of many search engines likes Google, Bing, Yahoo, *etc.*, validate the maturity level of vector space model as vector space model and cosine distance are used to calculate the closeness of the files containing words and words provided in user's queries. Various techniques have been discussed by Baeza and Ribeiro [7] for parsing free text, indexing, clustering, classification, ranking and retrieval which utilize vector space model.

1.2.2 Metric Space Model

Metric space model is a model in which distances between all the objects of the set are defined. The distances, taken together, are called a metric on the set and distances are calculated by using distance measure functions which must follow the following four properties:

i. $d(x,y) \geq 0 \quad non-negativity,$

ii. $d(x,y) = 0 \quad iff \quad x = y \quad identity,$

iii. $d(x,y) = d(y,x) \quad symmetry, \, and$

iv. $d(x,z) \leq d(x,y) + d(y,z)$ *triangle inequality.*

1.2.2.1 Non-Metric Space Model

If datasets do not follow properties given in metric space model, such dataset are considered in non-metric space. In most of the cases, datasets which are considered for non-metric space model are those which violate the triangle inequality, required for measuring the distance.

1.3 Probabilistic Data Structures for Similarity Search

Probabilistic Data Structures (PDS) are the advance data structures which use probabilistic approaches and approximation principles along with hashing techniques for fast processing of data [4]. PDS can be efficiently used in similarity search applications in comparison to deterministic data structures when data generated is so huge that every bit of data cannot be stored and deterministic data structures cannot be used efficiently. Hash functions used in PDS should be selected in such a way that they hash distinct items differently; leading to reduced error rate. The probability of error in different PDS varies according to number of parameters and number of hash functions used. Similarity search process using PDS show significant reduction in time and space complexity with marginal error probability, *i.e.*, with marginal cost of false positives and false negatives. Some of the important PDS which can be used for similarity search are:

1.3.1 Bloom Filter

Bloom Filter is a space efficient PDS used to represent a set $(S \subset U)$ of n elements. It consists of an array of m bits, denoted by $BF[1, 2, ...m]$, initially all bits set to *zero*. k independent hash functions are used to represent the data in a Bloom filter. It is assumed that the hash functions considered will map the elements independently in the universe to a random number uniformly over the range. For each element $X_i \in S$, bits $BF[h_j(X_i)]$ are set to *one*, $(\forall j|\ 1 < j < k.)$ Fig. 1.4 shows the insertion of elements in an array of m bits.

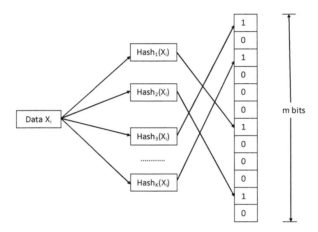

Figure 1.4: Insertion in Bloom filter

To check whether a query item, Y_i, is part of the data set or not, Y_i is first hashed and mapped with the $BF[1...m]$ array. If all hash positions in the Bloom array and Y_i are set to *one*, then Y_i is considered to be part of the corresponding data set. Fig. 1.5 depict the membership query in a Bloom filter corresponding to the Query item Y_i. Since number of elements inserted and the query time depends on number of hash functions, h, the time complexity of Bloom filter is $O(k)$.

The probability that a certain bit is not set to one by a hash function during the insertion of an element in the filter is $\frac{1}{m}$. With k hash functions, probability of specific bits not set to one is $(1 - \frac{1}{m})^k$. The probability of given bit being set to zero after n insertions is:

$$\left(1 - \frac{1}{m}\right)^{kn} \tag{1.7}$$

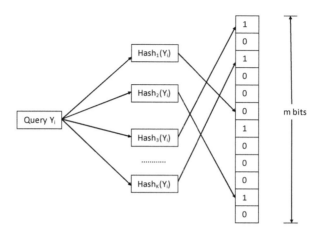

Figure 1.5: Query in Bloom filter

The probability of that bit being set to one is:

$$1 - \left(1 - \frac{1}{m}\right)^{kn} \tag{1.8}$$

There is always a probability of false positives in Bloom filter, *i.e.*, a particular element may not be the part of array but Bloom array may claim it to be part of the array. Probability of false positive f_p is:

$$f_p = \left(1 - \left(1 - \frac{1}{m}\right)^{kn}\right)^k \tag{1.9}$$

Using approximation principle, false positive probability, f_p is:

$$f_p \approx (1 - e^{-kn/m})^k \tag{1.10}$$

False positive rate [8] of Bloom filter can be minimize by taking optimal values of m and k

$$k_{opt} = \ln(2) \times \frac{m}{n} \tag{1.11}$$

$$m = \frac{k \times n}{ln(2)} \qquad (1.12)$$

Although Bloom filter stores data compactly for membership test it can be efficiently used for approximate similarity matching of two documents. Since Bloom filter produces some false positive errors, it is not suited for exact similarity match but can be optimally used for near exact matches. Bloom filter is generally used in sequential manner but it supports parallel execution too. Several applications in networks, distributed databases, dictionaries, *etc.*, are using Bloom filters.

1.3.2 Variants of Bloom Filter for Similarity Search

This subsection discusses few variants of Bloom filter used in similarity search of textual data.

1.3.2.1 Matrix Bloom Filter

Matrix Bloom filter (MBF), introduced by Geravand and Ahmadi [9], is a variant of standard Bloom filter for plagiarism detection. In MBF, every document is parsed and substrings generated are hashed as a unique row in the MBF. Thus, each row of MBF represents a document in a m-bit Bloom filter array. Query document is parsed and hashed where comparison is performed between query item and every row of the MBF through a bitwise AND operation. The number of bits set to *one* in each row indicate the similarity score of the query document with every document considered for comparison. Fig. 1.6 shows the logical representation of MBF where each row represent the document in the form of Bloom filter [10].

1.3.2.2 Bloofi

Bloofi [1] is a hierarchical structure of Bloom filters in which root (top level) Bloom filter stores the union of contents of their child node and this process is used recursively. All the Bloom filters having data elements associated with them stay at leaf level whereas all intermediate and root Bloom filters are used to store support information to reduce the access time and thus increase the performance of the proposed scheme.

Bits→ Docs↓	b_1	b_2	b_3	.	.	.	b_m
D_1							
D_2							
D_3							
...							
D_n							

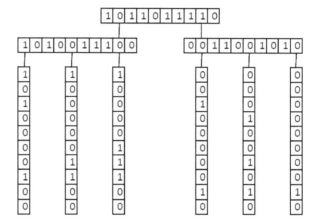

Figure 1.6: Matrix Bloom Filter

Figure 1.7: Bloofi Tree [1]

1.3.2.3 Sequence Bloom Tree

A data structure similar to Bloofi has been proposed by Solomon and Kingsford called Sequence Bloom Tree (SBT) [2] which is used for storing short read sequences. In SBT all leaf nodes store the data whereas root and intermediate nodes store the union of their child node. The main advantage of using SBT is that it accelerates the searching of query sequence, Fig. 1.8 depicts the SBT.

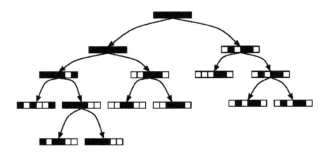

Figure 1.8: Sequence Bloom Tree [2]

1.3.3 Min Hash

Similarity search on large datasets, containing tera bytes of data, need computationally efficient and reliable data structures. Calculating the intersection and union of sets is very time consuming process and it becomes almost infeasible when number of sets are in millions. One of the alternative is a hashing based sampling algorithm called Min Hash (MH). It uses min-wise independent permutations by using multiple hash functions to calculate similarity among sets. It is an approximate version of Jaccard Similarity (discussed in Section 1.2) used for calculating the similarity among sets.

In MH similarity between members of a set $S = s_1, s_2, ...s_n$ is performed by mapping of k hash functions $H_k(S) \mapsto Z$. The minimum value from the set of hash function $h_{min} \leftarrow min(H_k(.))$ is stored in h_{min}. Two elements s_1 and s_2 of set S are considered similar if $h_{min}(s_1) = h_{min}(s_2)$ [11].

$$Pr[h_{min}(s_1) = h_{min}(s_2)] \Rightarrow \frac{|s_1 \cap s_2|}{|s_1 \cup s_2|} \approx J(s_1, s_2) \qquad (1.13)$$

If mH is a random variable, similarity of two items s_1 and s_2 is given by:

$$mH = \begin{cases} 1, & \text{if } h(s_1) = h(s_2) \\ 0, & \text{otherwise} \end{cases} \qquad (1.14)$$

Here $mH \in (0, 1)$ is unbiased estimator of similarity.

In Min hash, massive data is compressed in the form of a signature matrix and pairwise comparison is performed using Locality Sensitive Hashing (LSH) to identify the pairs of similar items in the dataset.

1.3.3.1 Steps in Min Hash

Shingling

Shingle is a process of breaking down the text into a sub-sequence of tokens of length k where size of k varies according to application being considered. Basically it is a pre processing technique to accommodate the data in a compressed form leading to space saving.

Characteristic Matrix (CM)

Shingles generated in the previous step are hashed and jaccard similarity is computed. The matrix set generated where rows represent the values of shingles and columns represent the documents is called *characteristic matrix*.

Signature Matrix (SM)

SM is generated by the usage of a hash function $\phi(.)$, randomly picked from a row generated from CM and permutation of the rows across the columns to generate more random results. a $(m \times n)$ signature matrix is generated by repetition of this process m times.

1.3.4 Locality-Sensitive Hashing

Locality-Sensitive Hashing (LSH) is used for solving the approximate nearest neighbor or exact near neighbor in $\Re^d$ space where d is very large [12]. The key idea behind LSH is to employ hash functions such that the probability of collisions become much higher for objects close to each other than for those that are far apart. The behavior of hashing in LSH is different from normal hashing in the sense that in case of normal hashing, items may go far apart after applying hash function that were close before hashing but in case of LSH, items maintain their closeness even after hashing. Fig. 1.9 provides comparison of general hashing with LSH; in general hashing items are mapped randomly, whereas in LSH similar type of items are hashed to same bucket.

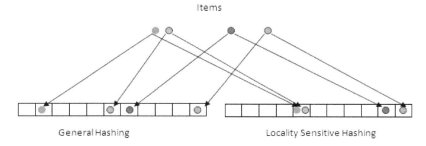

Figure 1.9: Comparison of General Hashing and LSH [3]

With a set of n points, d dimensions and H set of hash functions, mapping $\Re^d \to U_s$ data set to some universe for $x_i \in \Re^d | 1 < i < n$; two points $x_i, x_j \in \Re^d$ select hash function s.t., $(\exists h \in H)$ and analyze the probability of $h(x_i) = h(x_j)$. Let D be the distance measure for pair of $x_i, x_j \in \Re^d$, d_1 and d_2 be two distance ranges between any pair of $x_i, x_j \in \Re^d$ then P_1 and P_2 are the probabilities that x_i and x_j will reside in same bucket. The family of H is called locality sensitive or $(d_1, d_2, P_1, P_2)-$ sensitive [12].

A family H of hash functions is said to be $(d_1, d_2, P_1, P_2)-$sensitive if:

- $D||x_i, x_j|| \leq d_1$ then $Pr_H[h(x_i) = h(x_j)] \geq P_1$
- $D||x_i, x_j|| \geq d_2$ then $Pr_H[h(x_i) = h(x_j)] \leq P_2$

for all cases $d_1 < d_2$ and all queries satisfy $P_1 > P_2$, here $D||x_i, x_j||$ denotes the distance between two points. If x_i and x_j are close in $\Re^d$ space, i.e., $D||x_i, x_j||$ is less then there is high probability that P_1 will reside in the same group. The same has been illustrated in Fig. 1.10.

LSH operates in three steps: initial stage called pre-processing maps data through different distance measures, in next step hash tables are generated though a step called hash generation, and in the last step, similarity is searched where hash tables identify similar items. Entire data is placed in n buckets such that similar items are placed in same bucket. The detailed operations of LSH are illustrated in Fig. 1.11.

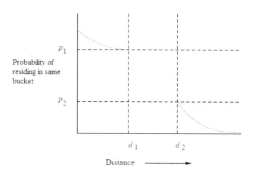

Figure 1.10: Probability *vs.* distance measure in LSH

1.4 Similarity Search Approaches

Retrieval of similar items corresponding to the query item is quite easy if the dataset size is small. Brute-force algorithms can compute the similarity scores and sort the data in ascending order and top k items are provided as results. As the size of datasets increases, linear search algorithms become inefficient. To overcome the limitations of linear methods, partitioning and approximation based similarity search methods are preferred to support fast processing.

1.4.1 Partitioning

In partition based approaches, data is divided into multiple partitions and at the search time only selected partition(s) are searched and remaining partitions are skipped thus it reduces the search space and provide fast access. Several tree and cluster based approaches support this type of retrieval. Partition based approaches are limited to low dimensional data (10 to 20). Kd-tree [13] is one of the common data structure used for partition based retrieval. As the dimensionality of data increases, tree based approaches begin to show their limits. To overcome the issue due to high dimensional data, approximate solutions are proposed in literature which give fast results.

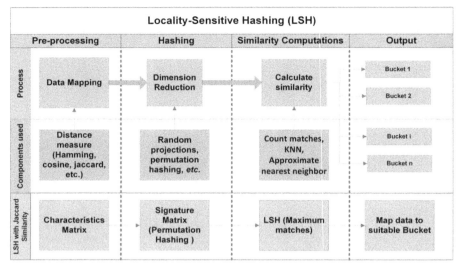

Figure 1.11: Locality-Sensitive Hashing Framework [4]

1.4.2 Approximation

The idea of approximate solution in various similarity search algorithms has been developed for the applications having high-dimensional data and the relaxation of correctness can be taken. The aim of approximate solutions is to reduce the processing time by relaxing the correctness constraint. Indyk and Motwani [12] proposed Locality-Sensitive Hashing to index hamming space data in sub-linear time. Further, Datar *et al.* extended LSH for L_p norms in [14]. The similarity search approaches in which Bloom filters are used (Section 1.6.2), feature vectors of original dataset are represented by Bloom filters after applying the hashing process on the feature vectors.

1.5 Similarity Search using GPU

With the growth of data size and complexity it was realized that the standalone systems will not be able to process data effectively. To overcome the issues related to the serial computation, parallel computing came into existence to process large volume of data

[15]. Parallel processing for similarity search can be achieved on multiple processors, thereby reducing processing time. In this work GPU has been used to for parallel computing.

1.5.1 GPU Computing

The use of Graphics Processing Units for non-graphical applications is growing rapidly due to the high computing capacity of these graphics cards for Massive Parallel Processing (also known as Data-Level Parallelism) at reasonable cost [16]. GPU follows Single Instruction and Multiple Data (SIMD) programming model. For efficiency, GPU uses a single program called kernel, to process multiple data items in parallel. GPU based implementations do not reduce the program complexity, but due to massive parallel processing it reduces the overall processing time [17]. One of the major requirements in such programming models is that all data items must be independent of each other. Several similarity search approaches have been using GPU based parallelism [18, 19, 20, 21].

1.5.2 Compute Unified Device Architecture (CUDA)

CUDA is a parallel computing platform and programming model that enables dramatic increase in computing performance by harnessing the power of GPUs. Since its introduction in 2006, CUDA has been widely used in many applications and supported by many devices such as laptops, workstations, mobiles, *etc.* Applications in astronomy, biology, chemistry, physics, data mining, manufacturing, finance, and other computationally intense fields are increasingly using CUDA to deliver the benefits of GPU acceleration. Some important concepts of CUDA are:

Kernels: A CUDA program runs in heterogeneous environment, *i.e.*, CPU and GPU. Program's execution starts with CPU. The data and the control is transferred to GPU where the kernel code runs in SIMD mode and the result is copied back to the CPU.

Thread Hierarchy: Arrangement of GPU processing units is divided into Grid, Block and Thread. A grid consists of multiple blocks and a block has multiple threads. Each thread is capable of executing a kernel code. Placement of number of threads and blocks for kernel code according to the number of processing units is very important for efficient utilization of GPU.

Memory Coalescing: Combining threads into warps is not only important for fast computation, but also useful for accessing global memory. GPU coalesces the global memory; loads and stores memory addresses generated by threads of a warp.

1.6 Role of Similarity Search in Data Intensive Applications

In various organizations, data-driven applications play a crucial role for several decision making processes. These applications require similarity search approaches to extract useful information from the large and complex datasets. This section discusses few applications which utilize similarity search partially or fully.

1.6.1 Document Clustering

Document clustering is the process of partitioning a large collection of documents into various groups. The similarity of any pair of the documents is high if they belong to the same cluster. To perform clustering of documents, pair wise distance needs to be computed among all the document and based on the distance and number of clusters, documents are arranged into groups. Computing similarity between every pair is quite time consuming but many researchers have tried to provide efficient solutions using PDS [22]. Zamora *et al.* [23] introduced LSH based clustering which provide relaxation on similarity computation. SimHash [24] and MinHash [11] hashing principles have been used to compute the approximate similarity instead of Jaccard and Cosine similarity. To further improve the search time, similarity is computed on Hamming space which required comparatively less computational time. Viegas *et al.* [25] proposed an automatic document classification system which uses Lazy Semi Naive Bayes approach. This approach support parallelism using GPU to accelerate the process.

Document clustering is used in social networks for categorization and annotation. It is used as a core operation for automatic spam filtering and content organization in multiple groups.

1.6.2 Plagiarism Detection

It is a process of identifying copied contents within a textual document. The easy availability of content on the Internet has increased the cases of plagiarism in different forms. It is now easier to plagiarize the work of others, especially in academia, where documents are typically research article, essays or reports. The state-of-the-art approaches focus on better accuracy of similarity detection of copied contents. Geravand and Ahmadi [10] proposed a plagiarism detection system which uses Matrix Bloom filter (MBF) to represent the documents.

1.6.3 Recommender System

Recommender Systems help users to explore items of interest from a collection of resources. Various e-commerce websites, social networking platforms, entertainment sources, *etc.*, use recommender systems to provide relevant results to the user by analysing their past interests [26]. This automatic recommendation process is based on user-user, user-item or item-item similarity. Recommender systems, which are part of publisher houses like Elsevier, Springer, IEEE, *etc.*, suggest the articles similar to the article downloaded by the users . Few online services such as Elsevier Journal Finder, Springer Journal Suggester, EndNote Manuscript Matcher, *etc.*, use title and abstract of a paper to recommend journals. The recommended list of journals are based on the similarity between the contents of the paper and associated text of the journals [27].

1.6.4 Health Care System

Similarity search play an important role in obtaining insights from Hospital Information Systems [28]. Mining hospitals data can help in providing directions for new discoveries and improve efficiency and communication within hospital systems. Majority of the valuable information in hospital records is represented in free text format, like radiology and pathology reports, requiring the application of text mining and natural language processing techniques. One of the important constraint in identifying similar health records of patient is to protect the privacy of the patient's records. Randall *et al.* [29] proposed an idea which uses Bloom filter based similarity search to link the similar records. The benefit of using Bloom filter is that it preserves the privacy while process the sensitive information. Apart from privacy issue, Bloom filter based approaches are also fast.

1.6.5 Fingerprints Matching

With the advancement in image processing, fingerprints have been widely used for person's recognition. Fingerprints are used for biometric recognition because they are unique and invariant and it is a well known fact that although the size of a fingerprint may change, the pattern of ridge shapes, ridge number and other features remain unchanged [30]. Nowadays, fingerprint authentication systems are widely used in mobile devices, banks and various financial institutions. One of the world's largest biometric database system, UIDAI uses fingerprints as biometric recognition.

1.6.6 Face Recognition

Face recognition is an important application of similarity search where human identity verification is done through a person's facial contour. In this process, comparison is done between user's facial contour and existing database. One of the major challenge here is to accurately recognize millions of faces with unique identities. These systems are useful in application like security systems, image gallery, gaming, *etc.*

1.7 Thesis Organization

Thesis has been organized into following chapters:

Chapter 1: Introduction

This chapter provides an overview of similarity search approaches, various distance measures used for similarity calculation, probabilistic data structures used for similarity search along with the application domains where similarity search is desired.

Chapter 2: Literature Review

This chapter provides a brief overview of approximate and parallel retrieval approaches for high dimensional datasets. Further, various approaches and applications specific to textual and non-textual dataset are reviewed. This chapter concludes with the problem formulation and objectives of the thesis.

Chapter 3: A Parallel Computational Approach for Similarity Search using Bloom Filters (PCASSB)

In this chapter, a similarity search approach is proposed for computing similarity of textual documents in parallel using GPU. To accomplish the task, initially documents are converted into feature vectors and the extracted feature vectors are mapped to Bloom filters to represent the documents. Further these documents are compared with query documents in parallel using GPU.

Chapter 4: Similarity Search Approaches for Image Datasets

In this chapter, two CBIR approaches: An Efficient Bi-layer Content Based Image Retrieval System (BiCBIR) and Efficient Feature Incremental Approach for Content Based Image Retrieval System (FiCBIR) are proposed. The proposed approaches consist of two modules: feature extraction and image retrieval corresponding to the query image. Features are extracted in the form of color, texture and shape, and retrieval process is further divided into layers, two layers in BiCBIR and three layers in FiCBIR.

Chapter 5: Implementation Details and Results

This chapter discusses the implementation environment used for the proposed CBIR approaches. Further, the results achieved are discussed at length. Results have been evaluated on the basis of precision, recall and f-score evaluation metrics and compared with various state-of-the art techniques.

Chapter 6: Conclusion and Future Scope

Work done in this research is concluded in this chapter and major contributions of the thesis have been discussed. Further, this chapter provides the future directions in similarity search for text and image datasets.

Chapter 2

Literature Review

This chapter provides the review of similarity search approaches related to textual and non-textual dataset. The review is broadly based on feature extraction methods and retrieval approaches.

Similarity search is one of the essential and computationally expensive operation of data intensive applications which involves searching of the most similar objects in high-dimensional vectors [31]. The retrieval process in these application is challenging task, especially when it needs to be accomplished in minimum time and space. There is always a trade-off between time and space to design an algorithm for retrieval process. To make the retrieval process faster, parallelism is one of the option which is commonly used when data under consideration is very large and independently processed. Approximate solutions are another interesting way which utilize accuracy-time trade-off. In this process exhaustive searching process is avoided while maintaining the acceptable accuracy which varies from application to application. In various applications such as Plagiarism checking, Mirror pages searching, Fingerprint matching, *etc.*, approximate solutions are suited well.

2.1 Approximate Similarity Search

Approximate similarity search has the goal of reducing the cost of similarity queries by relaxing the correctness constraint, *i.e.*, the k items in the approximate result might not be the closest to the query item q. Since applications deal with unstructured text datasets, they datasets must be preprocessed and feature vectors should be formed before the similarity computation task begin. It also require preprocessing of query text along with some other task such as query expansion, indexing, *etc.* In the process of similarity search, a pair-wise similarity score between query text and list of documents is computed. The distance or similarity measure functions are used to compute the similarity score.

Various metric, non-metric and vector space models have been proposed for similarity search. A survey by Skopal and Bustos discusses several domains and effective similarity search techniques in non-metric space [32]. There are many tree-based indexing schemes for Nearest Neighbor search or similarity search which include k-d trees [13], navigating nets [33], cover trees [34], r-trees [35], and sr-trees [36], *etc.* These techniques perform well for low dimensional datasets but fail to cope up with high dimensional feature space. When massive data sets are under consideration, use of probabilistic data structure is one of the best available options.

Bloom filter based algorithms are used in various applications where distributed databases or cache membership protocols can be efficiently used. Since Bloom filters use only one small bit array, to identify whether the given data item exists at a server or not, one needs to check only a small bit array (Bloom filter) locally, without querying the remote database [37].

Sairam *et al.* [38] proposed a technique for similarity search on encrypted dataset by using modified Jaccard similarity where Bloom filters were used for representing datasets and similarity was calculated. Jain *et al.* used duplicate detection technique based on Bloom filter which evaluated similarity between query results to eliminate or reorganize duplicate web pages. They evaluated the proposed technique on search engines like Google, MSN and Yahoo [39].

Sandor *et al.* [40] proposed a data structure, called EGH filter, which provides basic Bloom filter operations and the operations supported are free from false positive cases for finite universe and limited number of items. Hua *et al.* proposed an algorithm, Locality-Sensitive Bloom filter (LSBF) which improves approximate membership query

[41]. This algorithm uses locality sensitive hashing functions instead of uniform and independent hash functions in Bloom filter. Using LSH functions in Bloom filter, elements are stored locally thus can be searched quickly. To reduce false positive they used an extra small size Bloom filter which verifies the Approximate Membership Query (AMQ) query result.

Luo *et al.* introduced an Invertible Counting Bloom filter (ICBF) for multiset synchronization [42], built on top of Counting Bloom filter (CBF) and Invertible Bloom filter (IBF) which had an inherent limitation that they can deal only with simple set synchronization. ICBF overcame this limitation and supported multiset synchronization efficiently. Since Naive Bayes approach is not quite efficient in terms of time and accuracy for document classification, in [25] Viegas *et al.* introduced a Semi Lazy Naive Bayes technique for document classification which expedited the process of Automatic Document Classification (ADC) by exploiting Naive Bayes assumption that the data is independent.

To process huge amount of unstructured text data for data incentive task, Term Frequency-Inverse Document Frequency (TF-IDF) is widely used technique to find the usability of data. But when data is in form of continues stream, traditional TF-IDF is not suitable due to limited memory and time constraint. To overcome such issues Erra *et al.* [43] proposed a parallel approximate version of TF-IDF by using GPU. Mu *et al.* proposed a GPU based solution for the IP routing applications such as table lookup and pattern matching which are quite time consuming processes [44]. They implemented Bloom filter based string matching algorithm for deep packet inspection in the network.

Indyk and Motwani have shown that for sufficiently high dimensions, all available partitioning schemes downgrades to linear search or show only little improvement over linear search. To overcome such issues they proposed Locality-Sensitive Hashing [12] which is linearly dependent on the size of data. Instead of partitioning method, it uses several hashing methods to hash the points to increase the probability of collision for objects which are similar than for those which are not. Near neighbors can be determined by hashing the queried point and retrieving those elements stored in buckets that contain those points. The major drawback of LSH is that it performs well only for Hamming space. Broder et al. [45] designed an LSH scheme based on Jaccard similarity of sets which uses Minhash functions to take different permutations to calculate Jaccard similarity for sets [11]. To improve the performance and usability several optimal parameters for LSH have been proposed by Slaney [46]. Normally hash functions used in LSH generate hash table randomly. In order to get high quality results, multiple hash tables are generated which take extra space and increase execution time. To overcome these inefficacies, Jin et al. [47] proposed a novel hashing algorithm called Density Sensitive Hashing (DSH). It generates less number of hash tables as compared to LSH. DSH exploits the geometric features of the data to avoid the total random mapping. Mapping functions are selected on the basic of distribution of the data.

2.2 Similarity Search through Parallel Processing

In the late 1970s, computing industry witnessed a change from file based storage system to the database management system for effective storage, retrieval, search, and analysis. With the growth of data volume in these systems, it was realised that single machine such as mainframe computer will not be able to process data effectively in spite of its enormous processing power. To overcome the issues related to the single mainframe machine, in the 1980s, the notion of parallel database systems based on 'share nothing' concept came up to process large volume of data [15]. In these parallel databases systems every machine had its own CPU, memory and disk. In the late 1990s, parallel database systems were widely accepted by the industry.

Stupar et al. proposed an approach for implementation of LSH termed as RankReduce, which can be employed for similarity search in high dimensional data on MapReduce infrastructure [48]. In their proposed approach, MapReduce and LSH are utilized for achieving high accuracy and exceptional performance. MapReduce is not employed for query processing but to process huge volume of data online. Zhang et al. exploited the parallelism of GPU for text mining by creating hash tables since traditional clustering methods are not capable of clustering streaming data like tweets, news articles, blogs, etc. [49].

Szaszy and Samet [50] propounded a parallel online clustering algorithm to cluster streaming data. Pan et al. [51] introduced LSH and Cuckoo hashing based k-Nearest Neighbor (kNN) search which use GPU parallelism effectively for motion planning to compute proximity. Pan and Manocha [52] proposed an algorithm for R^d spaces where parallel LSH algorithm was used for approximate kNN and parallelism was achieved by GPU. They used Bi-level LSH technique, which can calculate kNN with higher accuracy and is amenable to parallelization. In level one, they partitioned datasets in a way that items similar to each other were clustered together, for which a parallel RP-tree algorithm was used. Level two constructed a hierarchical hash table by considering each item and generating the Bi-Level LSH code.

Ma et al. [53] implemented a fast version of BLAST for genome bio-sequence alignment on GPUs and defined a measure for quantifying the trade-offs between performance and false positive rates. For this purpose they developed an analytical performance model that helps in increasing the usage of Bloom filters. Ong et al. implemented LSH using parallel Bloom filter over serial Bloom filter for string searching algorithms [54] where the parallel Bloom filter algorithm has been designed using CUDA, a parallel computing platform. The algorithm generated a bit table by segmenting the input string list into block of words. The algorithm demonstrated significant improvement over serial Bloom filter implementation.

Teitler et al. [55] proposed a parallel clustering algorithm using GPUs to parallelize the computation of TF-IDF. They provided two variant of parallel clustering algorithms: first algorithm clustered single documents in parallel and second algorithm performed clustering of multiple document in parallel. Bloom filter based similarity search is used for privacy preserving record linkage used in many real-world health care systems by different countries such as Australia, Brazil, Germany and Switzerland. Randall et al. introduced a Bloom filter based method suitable for large-scale linkage of patient records [29]. Hwang et al. implemented parallel version of DUST [56] using GPU in which they performed probability computations to accelerate the performance of initial version of DUST [57]. To identify structural similarity in exponentially growing protein dataset, Mrozek *et al.* proposed a GPU based CASSERT technique named GPU-CASSERT [17].

Iacob *et al.* employed GPUs in information retrieval where response time is an important factor; similarity of documents to the query document was calculated by first representing the documents in a Bloom filters and then comparison was performed with query Bloom filter and documents in parallel. Their methodology demonstrated significant reduction in search time [19]. Gowanlock and Casanova [58] proposed distance threshold based similarity search where all trajectories of a query trajectory were identified by using a large number of Euclidean calculations within a given distance over a time interval. They demonstrated that their proposed technique executes well with GPUs.

The similarity between two audio fingerprints can be stated as the intersection between their elements. Searching over millions of fingerprints data is a challenging task since it involves high dimensionality. Ouali *el al.* investigated the database of fingerprints to reduce the search time for finding the identical fingerprints by using GPU [18, 21, 59]. Dunn *et al.* used GPU to compute document similarity in automated bug triaging process for different software bug repositories [60].

2.3 Similarity Search in Text based Applications

In various applications such as plagiarism detection, web pages searching, document clustering, *etc.*, similarity search plays an essential role. These applications help in decision making based on data insights rather than heuristics. To retrieve the useful information from textual data, these applications rely on similarity search [61].

Broadly, similarity search can be divided into two parts; feature extraction and similarity computation. Feature extraction techniques have been used in text based information retrieval such as shingles, bag of words and content defined chucking. To measure the similarity of the documents based on the features extracted, various distance measure functions are available (Section 1.1).

2.3.1 Text Features Extraction Techniques

In this section, various feature extraction techniques to retrieve textual features are discussed.

2.3.1.1 Shingling

Shingling is a feature extraction approach which is used to represent the text documents into feature vectors. It breaks a document into a set of items and these items form a feature vector. Based on the application, shingles can be extracted on the basis of characters, phonemes, syllables, words, *etc.*

2.3.1.2 Bag of Words (BOW)

Bag of words (BOW) model is a way of representing text data when modeling text with machine learning algorithms. The BoW model is simple to understand and implement and has seen great success in problems such as language modeling and document classification.

2.3.1.3 Content Defined Chucking (CDC)

Content Defined Chucking (CDC) break the large text document into smaller and variable size of chunks, with a property to recognize the same chunks within the file or in other files. This enables restriction to de-duplicate on the level of chunks. CDC is useful in applications, such as data compression and data synchronization [62].

2.3.2 Summary of Text Retrieval Approaches

Summary of the similarity search approaches have been provided in Table 2.1. The summary consists of feature extraction technique used by particular researcher, support for parallelism, data structure used, application area where the proposed technique can be used and the dataset used for testing.

Table 2.1: Comparisons of various text based similarity search approaches

Authors	Features	Parallelism	Data Structure	Distance measure	Application	Dataset considered
Schnel et al. [63]	q-Grams	No	Bloom filter	Dice coefficient	Patient record linkage	German private administration databases
Randall et al. [29]	q-Grams	No	Bloom filter	Dice coefficient	Patient record matching	West Australian Hospital Admissions Data and New South Wales Admitted Patient Data
Jain et al. [64]	CDC	Yes	Bloom filter	Hamming	Web page retrieval	Web search results
Iacob et al. [19]	BoW	Yes	Bloom filter	Cosine	Information retrieval	UCI-bioinformatics, molecular physics, astronomy
Vatsalan et al. [65]	q-Grams	No	Bloom filter	Dice coefficient	Patient record matching	Breast Cancer and Diabetes, and one Medical Quality Improvement Consortium
Geravand and Ahmadi [10]	Document chunks	No	Matrix Bloom filter	Bit-wise AND	Plagiarism checking system	2000 Journals
Cotelo et al. [66]	BoW	No	-	Dice coefficient	Tweet categorization	Political Tweets
Zamora et al. [23]	Term	No	LSH	Hamming	Data Clustering	Department of energy documents and 20Newsgroup
Zhang et al. [67]	-	No	Multi-index structure	Hamming	Indexing	Corela, SIFT, Audio and Aerial
Zhou et al. [68]	LSTM	No	-	Hamming	Text retrieval	IMDB, YELP13 and YELP14
Sohrabi and Azgomi [69]	-	Yes	LSH	Jaccard	Similarity Join	DBLP and APD
Fuentes-Pineda and Meza-Ruiz [70]	-	No	LSH	Min-hash	Topic Discovery	Reuters corpus and 20Newsgroup

2.4 Similarity Search in Images

With the availability of image capturing devices, like smart phones, digital cameras, closed circuit television camera, *etc.*, huge volumes of visual data is generated. Millions of images are uploaded on the social networking websites in a single day [71]. At the beginning image retrieval system were based on Query By Text (QBT) [72, 73]. In QBT image retrieval systems search was performed by providing the textual queries. The problem with such system is that retrieval is possible if each and every image is annotated. Another problem is the visual data uploaded by users from various geographic regions with varied languages have either meta data in diverse languages or no meta data associated with the images [74]. Due to aforementioned issues QBT techniques are not effective. Another major concern in image search systems is that an image can have many versions which differ in size or color and it can be seen from different view points, thus making it hard to compare the images pixel by pixel. To avoid mismatch due to rotation, translation, scaling, *etc.*, features of the images should be extracted to compute the similarity among images [75]. The searching of images based on image features (content) is known as Content Based Image Retrieval (CBIR). A CBIR system is mainly affected by: i) image feature selection and extraction technique ii) number of features used to represent the image iii) similarity measure methods used to compute the similarity between two images and iv) retrieval methods used for searching of images from the image dataset [72]. In literature, there are many surveys and reviews that analyze these steps in detail [74, 76, 77, 78, 79]. In the coming subsection, CBIR approaches are discussed based on types of features used to represent the image, methods to improve the accuracy of CBIR systems by merging various image features, and retrieval approaches used to reduce the search time.

2.4.1 Image Features Extraction

An important concern with CBIR systems is the semantic gaps [80, 81] among high-level image concepts and low-level image features. Generally image searching approaches use low level features which include color, texture, shape, *etc.*, to represent the images under consideration. Image features can be global or local. Global features describe an image as a whole and can be interpreted as a particular property of the image involving all pixels, whereas local features detect key points or region of interest in an image to describe the same. Global features have fast retrieval rate but they are not effective in comparing region of interest [82, 83]. Local features [84, 85] of images are invariant to translation, rotation, scale, *etc*. There are several image feature extraction approaches proposed in literature and some of them are discussed here. There are several image retrieval systems which retrieve similar images on the basis of image features, also known as image contents [80, 86].

The Bag-of-Visual-Words (BoVW) is widely used image feature representation method [87] in many applications of computer vision [88]. BoVW model is a standard approach to map local features into a vector of fixed length [89]. Feature vectors are quantized into visual words formulated by clustering the image features [90]. To avoid high computation involved in image segmentation, Jian *et al.* [91] introduced a perception based directional patch extraction and salient patch detection method to extract local features for CBIR. It is important to use primitive image features in CBIR to tackle the versatile image datasets [92]. Yue *et al.* [93] considered color histogram for color feature and co-occurrence matrix for texture feature extraction. Further, weights were assigned to color and texture feature. Pradhan *et al.* [94] proposed a CBIR framework which uses adaptive tetrolet transform for texture feature extraction. Color and shape features are extracted by using color channel correlation histogram and edge joint histogram, respectively. Tong *et al.* [95] proposed an algorithm for image retrieval based on granular computing. The advantage of the proposed approach was that it worked efficiently in case of disordered image information.

2.4.2 Feature Merging

Feature merging is the process of combining two or more feature vectors to form a single feature vector. The combination of primitive features such as the color, texture and shape provide a robust features set for image retrieval [82, 96, 97]. Dey *et al.* [98] proposed a CBIR system which uses fusion of color and texture features. They applied two-level discrete wavelet transform to extract texture features. Wang et al. [82] proposed a CBIR scheme by merging the three most common features, i.e., color, texture and shape of an image, which gives comparatively better retrieval accuracy [82, 99]. Zhou et al. [100] merged color histogram, local directional pattern and dense Scale Invariant Feature Transform (SIFT) features to represent the images more accurately. Fadaei et al. [101] proposed a CBIR scheme which uses color and texture features for image representation. In this scheme, uniform partitioning was applied on HSV color space to extract Dominant Color Descriptor (DCD) features. Texture features were extracted by using wavelet and curvelet to avoid noise and translation problems associated with image retrieval. Color and texture features were combined by assigning optimal weights with the help of particle swarm optimization. Due to order-less histogram generated by Bag of Visual Word (BoVW), spatial contents were ignored. To overcome the problem of BoVW, Mehmood et al. [102] proposed a Weighted Average of Triangular Histogram (WATH) for image representation. WATH included the spatial contents in the inverted index of BoVW model. Muhammad et al. [89] proposed CBIR approach which used features fusion technique of the SIFT and Local Intensity Order Pattern (LIOP) feature descriptors. Particle Swarm Optimization (PSO) algorithms have been used for feature weighting [103] and clustering [104] to enhanced the performance of CBIR system.

2.4.3 Content Based Image Retrieval

Two important aspects on which CBIR approaches focus are: i) image feature extraction and representation and ii) retrieval of similar images to the query image. Zhu et al. [105] proposed a CBIR system which consists of three steps: First step is preprocessing which uses manifold-ranking algorithm [106] to prune the irrelevant images. Similarity between query image and remaining images is computed by utilizing the probability density estimation is second step. Third step is a random walk with restart model, which is used to refine the ranking between query image and unlabeled images. Cheng et al. [107] proposed a multi-model aspect-aware topic model for recommender systems which uses text reviews and item images. Shao et al. [108] introduced supervised two-stage deep learning cross-modal retrieval which supports text to image and image to text retrieval. Garcia and Vogiatzis [109] introduced a non-metric similarity computation method based on neural network. Deep learning based image features have been recently proposed by Wang *et al.* [110] in which top layer image features are used in CBIR instead of intermediate layer image features leading to fast retrieval with high accuracy. Heidy *et al.* [111] proposed an image annotation scheme, based on chain classifiers, which employs ensemble approach for classifier in the supervised image annotation. Each model in the chain deals with the same classification problem, making the proposed method an ensemble model build from multi-modal data. Mezzoudj *et al.* [112] proposed a parallel k-NN search for CBIR system which uses Spark and MapReduce to speedup the indexing and searching process. Kokare *et al.* [113] introduced cosine modulated wavelet packet for texture feature extraction. This method has less computational cost and has good feature representation quality. Lai [114] proposed a color image retrieval scheme using Z-scanning technique for CBIR. Jenni *et al.* [115] proposed a CBIR approach which utilizes the support vector machine classifier. Features were extracted on the color string coding and string comparisons were used to retrieve similar images which reduced computational cost. Pavithra *et al.* [116] developed a hybrid framework for CBIR system to address the accuracy issues associated with the traditional image retrieval systems. The framework initially selected pertinent images from a large database using color moment information. Cui *et al.* [117] proposed a hybrid CBIR approach which used image tags and actual image contents to compute the relevancy of candidate images. To enhance the retrieval performance, missing image tags were generated and noisy tags were corrected. Islam *et al.* [118] proposed fuzzy based feature selection methods which combined the results of several rough-fuzzy methods for an image representation. Hashing based image retrieval systems are faster as compared to traditional CBIR systems but they are less accurate. To overcome the accuracy issues, Wang *et al.* [119] proposed a variational Bayes framework to learn robust hash code which provides better accuracy. Yan *et al.* [120] introduced a hashing based image retrieval method which utilized deep learning network to generate hash code for images. Yildizer *et al.* [121] proposed an ensemble approach which used multiple support vector machines. Feature vectors of images were generated by using Daubechies wavelet transform.

CBIR is a widespread technique applied in several applications such as bio-metric identification, digital libraries, homeland security, *etc.* Utilization of CBIR techniques for medical images has great potential for fast detection and diagnosis of various diseases [122, 123]. Existing methods studied in the literature require multiple scan of entire dataset. Further, these approaches require fusion and ranking to produce the final results. Moreover, such techniques require the appropriate weight assignment to different feature type. To avoid the aforementioned issues multi-layer CBIR approaches have been proposed which have fast retrieval and enhanced accuracy.

CBIR approaches also use Convolutional Neural Networks (CNN) based image features which provides better search results. Learning of CNN requires large number of annotated and domain specific sample images [124, 125]. With the availability of annotated image dataset in the recent years, CNNs can be trained to provide adequate level of generalization to image features [126]. Image features generated by CNNs are considered to be more robust as compared to hand-crafted ones [127, 128]. Since the success of Krizhevsky *et al.* [129] in the image classification, several CBIR approaches begin to utilize CNN based image features to provide better image search results. CNN has been successfully used in various computer vision domains such as image and video classification, food recognition [127], visual tracking [130], 3D object classification [131, 132], digit recognition [133], *etc.*

Some CBIR system uses multiple layers for feature matching and each layer compares only one feature. In multilayer setting, only selected images are passed to the next layer *i.e.* all irrelevant images are discarded [94, 134]. There are some CBIR systems [94, 134] which avoid exhaustive search by searching the entire dataset in three stages using three image features (color, texture and shape). In first stage, color feature is used to prune non-relevant images based on a particular feature space. In second stage, texture feature is used to prune out non-relevant images and finally in third stage, relevant images are retrieved using shape feature. In such layered approaches, images filtered after first stage of pruning are passed as input to second layer. Pradhan *et al.* [94] proposed a hierarchical CBIR system which utilizes three primitive image features and images similar to the query image are retrieved in three layers. In this CBIR system single feature is compared at each layer and based on the computed similarity only reduced set of images are compared at next layer. This layer wise approach allows searching on sub feature space which reduces the overall search time. Majority of studies on CBIR use combination of multiple image feature for similarity computation or subspace features space in multiple layers. Since different feature space is used in subsequent layers, similarity achieved in the first stage is lost and hence, some of relevant images may be dropped in second layer. Similarly, at third layer, images which are relevant for second layer but not for third layer feature space are dropped.

2.4.4 Summary of Image Retrieval Approaches

In this section, a summary of image retrieval approaches is given in Table 2.2 which consists of image features, feature extraction methods, application domain and involved dataset(s).

Table 2.2: Comparisons of various CBIR approaches based of features and retrieval methods

Authors	Feature	Feature Extraction Method	Retrieval Approach	Dataset
Salvi et al. [135]	CNN	1024d average pooling layer of GoogLeNet	Bloom filter based indexing has been used to support fast retrieval. Bloom filters used to discard searching in large feature dataset with out affecting the retrieval accuracy.	INRIA Holidays, Oxford 5K and Paris 6K
Fadaei et al. [136]	Texture	Local Derivative Radial Pattern (LDRP)	Texture features (LDRP) based image retrieval.	Brodatz and Vistex
Liu et al. [137]	Color and Texture	Color Information Feature (CIF) and Local Binary Pattern (LBP)	Fusion of CIF and LBP feature for image retrieval.	Brodatz and Vistex
Thiagarajan et al. [138]	Local and Global	Local:Local Binary Pattern, Global: Histogram of Oriented Gradients (HoG), and GIST,	Image retrieval based on fusion of local and global image features.	Microsoft Research Cambridge Image Dataset
Duanmu [139]	Color and Shape	Color moment invariant	Image retrieval based on color moment invariant features which combine color and shape information.	COIL-100
Wang et al. [140]	Color and Texture	Color: Pseudo-Zernike chromaticity distribution moments in opponent chromaticity space, and Texture: Rotation-invariant and scale-invariant image descriptor in steerable pyramid domain	CBIR method based on fusion of color and texture features.	COREL
Shao et al. [141]	Color	MPEG-7 dominant color descriptor	The Histogram intersection algorithm is used to measure similarity to retrieve the similar images.	COREL
Nazir et al. [142]	Color and Texture	Color: Color histogram, and Texture: Discrete wavelet transform and Edge histogram descriptor	CBIR technique to fuse color and texture features.	COREL-1000

Continued on next page

Table 2.2 – (Continued)

Authors	Feature	Feature Extraction Method	Retrieval Approach	Dataset
Ashraf et al. [143]	Color and Texture	Color: Color Moments, Texture: Gabor wavelet and Discrete wavelet transform, and Color and Edge Directivity Descriptor (CEDD)	CBIR technique to fuse the color and texture features along with CEDD.	COREL-1000
Liu et al. [144]	Color, Texture and Shape	Micro-structure descriptor	CBIR has high indexing performance and low dimensionality.	COREL-5000 and COREL-10000
Wang et al. [145]	Texture	Color co-occurrence matrix	CBIR using texture features.	COREL-1000 and COREL-10000
Li et al. [146]	Feature fusion	Product quantization (PQ) with sparse coding	Sketch-based image retrieval.	Eitz benchmark dataset
Mohamadzadeh and Farsi [147]	Color and Texture	Iterative discrete avelet transform	Image retrieval method based on sparse representation and iterative discrete wavelet transform.	Flower, COREL, Amsterdam Library of Object Image, VisTex and MPEG-7
Srinivas et al. [148]	Texture	Dictionary learning	Content-based medical image retrieval using clustering and dictionary learning.	ImageCLEF medical image dataset
Lasmar and Berthoumieu [149]	Texture	Gaussian copula-based multi-variate generalized gaussian, Gaussian copula-based multivariate Weibull	Image retrieval based on texture feature and Jeffrey divergence as a similarity measure.	Vistex, Brodatz and ALOT
Pandey and Khanna [99]	Color, Texture, Shape	HSV color histogram, Gabor filter, Pseudo zernike moments	Images are first clustered using agglomerative hierarchical clustering. Each cluster has representative image which is used to select the appropriate cluster for retrieval of images and clustering of other images.	ZuBuD, WANG, Caltech101 and UW

Continued on next page

Table 2.2 – (Continued)

Authors	Feature	Feature Extraction Method	Retrieval Approach	Dataset
Shrivastava and Tyagi [148]	Color, Texture, Shape	HSV color histogram, Gabor filter, Fourier coefficients	Hierarchical image retrieval approach has been used which have 3-level of hierarchy, in first level all the images are compared and relevant images passed to next level. In this hierarchical retrieval system, at every layer only one type of feature. The idea is to reduce the dataset at every layer to make retrieval process fast.	Corel and Cifar
Pradhan et al. [94]	Color, Texture, Shape	Color channel correlation histogram, Adaptive tetrolet transform, Joint edge histogram	Hierarchical retrieval approach similar to [134] but uses different feature extraction methods.	COREL, GHIM, COIL, PRODUCE, OLIVA and OUTEX

2.5 Problem Statement

One of the world's biggest data repository, World Wide Web, is a heterogeneous platform with various data formats; stored in the millions of servers spread world over. In this present petabyte age, traditional similarity search approaches have limited scope. Had the data been available in the form of tables as in relational databases or in a single defined format, searching would have been quite easy and efficient. But in today's digital universe when majority of data is non-text and feature-rich like images, audio, video, *etc.*, commonly available tools for identifying similar patterns cannot keep up with the increase in size, diversity and rate of change.

Various similarity search approaches have been suggested for identifying similar items in the high dimensional datasets but till date, there is no reported standard technique for providing a rationalized method for similarity search when data is arriving from various sources in the varied formats of text, images, videos, *etc.* The gravity of problem require new thinking to solve the similarity search problem in limited time and memory. The intent of this work is to develop some new similarity search techniques for textual and non-textual datasets which will optimize the retrieval performance of the desired information. In the proposed work our focus is twofold, first to use GPU for parallel processing and second to use approximate techniques to make retrieval process fast.

2.6 Research Objectives

1. To study, explore and analyse various tools, technologies and methodologies available for similarity search.

2. To propose and design similarity search techniques for textual and non-textual datasets.

3. To test and validate the proposed techniques using evaluation parameters like space complexity, time complexity, *etc.*

Chapter 3

A Parallel Computational Approach for Similarity Search using Bloom Filters (PCASSB)

In this work a combination of parallel and approximate processing has been used to identify similar items through the usage of Bloom filters in parallel. Coming sections discuss the proposed approach in detail.

3.1 Proposed approach

A Parallel Computational Approach for Similarity Search using Bloom Filter (PCASSB) is proposed which retrieves documents from the dataset similar to the user's query. PCASSB uses Bloom filter for document representation and Integer array for query representation. Broadly, the proposed similarity search approach is divided into two modules: Offline and Online. The pre-processing of documents is done in offline module and similarity of documents, based upon the user's query is computed in online module. The overview of the proposed approach is depicted in Fig. 3.1.

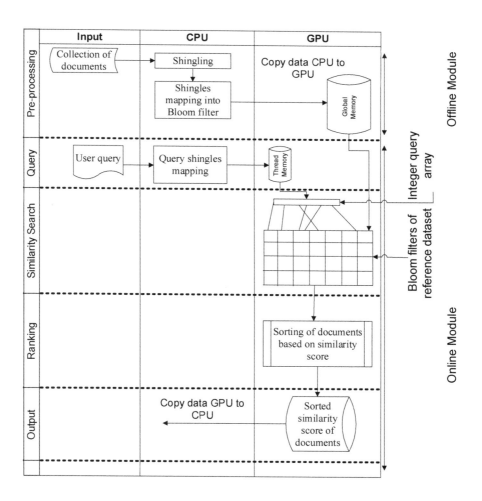

Figure 3.1: Framework of PCASSB

3.1.1 Offline Module

Offline module works in two phases: first phase is preprocessing of documents which involves conversion of documents into *sets* and next is creation of Bloom filters for the sets generated.

3.1.1.1 Preprocessing of Documents

The general approach followed to convert a document into a set is to shingle the document. Features are extracted from the dataset in the form of shingles. For a positive integer k and a sequence of terms in a document D, the k-shingles of D are defined as a set of all the successive sequences of k terms. k-shingles define a set of all k size non repeatable substrings of the document and group them as a single object. The set of k-shingles of a document with n words takes space O(kn). The space goes on decrease as items are repeated in the document. For example, if k=3 and a document contains text "This research work is related to similarity search" then the shingle's set will be { "This research work", "research work is", "work is related", "is related to", "related to similarity", "to similarity search"} The number k is selected based on the size of text file. It should be large enough so that repetition is least and small enough such that text file can be divided into units which can be easily compared. Preprocessing of documents $D = \{D_1, D_2 \ldots, D_n\}$ is performed on CPU side where stop words are removed and shingling is done to extract feature set from each document. For all the documents D in the dataset, shingle set S is generated where shingle set S^i represents the features of a document D_i.

3.1.1.2 Creation of Bloom Filters from Shingle Sets

Bloom filter of size m is filled by hashing elements of S^i using k hash functions and corresponding bits of hash indexes ($0 \geq index \geq (m-1)$) are set to 1 in Bloom filter

BF_i, i.e.

$$BF_i[H_g(S_j^i)] \leftarrow 1 \begin{cases} 0 <= i < |D| \\ 0 <= j < |S^i| \\ 0 <= g < k \end{cases} \quad (3.1)$$

Each shingles set S^i is represented by an individual Bloom filter BF_i where BF_d represent the $(|D|-1)^{th}$ document and $s_i = |S^i| - 1$ represents the shingles in i^{th} shingle set, such that:

$$BF_0 = \{b_{0,0}, b_{0,1}, \ldots b_{0,s_0}\}, b_{0,s_0} \in \{0,1\}$$
$$BF_1 = \{b_{1,0}, b_{1,1}, \ldots b_{1,s_1}\}, b_{1,s_1} \in \{0,1\}$$
$$\ldots$$
$$BF_i = \{b_{i,0}, b_{i,1}, \ldots b_{i,s_i}\}, b_{i,s_i} \in \{0,1\}$$
$$\ldots$$
$$\ldots$$
$$\ldots$$
$$BF_d = \{b_{d,0}, b_{d,1}, \ldots b_{d,s_i}\}, b_{d,s_i} \in \{0,1\}$$

These shingles *set*, represented as Bloom filter, are mapped to the GPU blocks. For each Bloom filter BF_i, four blocks are assigned in GPU. The mapping of shingle *sets* to Bloom filter is done using Algorithm 3.1.

Input: A set of Shingles $S = \{S^0, S^1, \ldots, S^n\}$ and Bloom filter BF^S
Output: BF^S with hashed values
1 **for** *i=0 to $|S|-1$* **do**
2   **foreach** S_j^i *in S^i* **do**
3   **for** *j=0 to k-1* **do**
4           $BF_i^S[H_j(S_j^i)] = 1$
5   **end**
6   **end**
7 **end**

Algorithm 3.1: Mapping of Shingle set to Bloom filter

3.1.2 Online Module

This module generates query results from the reference dataset and consists of the following three subtasks: (i) Query pre-processing, (ii) Similarity search and (iii) Ranking.

3.1.2.1 Query Pre-processing

In this task, when query Q is triggered, it is converted into shingles S_q which are further represented in the Integer Query Array ($^I Q_A$). Contents in $^I Q_A$ after hashing query items are:

$$^I Q_A \{ \underbrace{\{H_0(I_1), H_1(I_1), \ldots, H_{k-1}(I_1)\}}_{Item_1}, \underbrace{\{H_0(I_2), H_1(I_2), \ldots, H_{k-1}(I_2)\}}_{Item_2},$$
$$\ldots \underbrace{\{H_0(I_n), H_1(I_n), \ldots, H_{k-1}(I_n)\}}_{Item_n} \}$$

3.1.2.2 Similarity Search

In token based similarity search, similarity can be measure in two ways: Symmetric Similarity Computation (SSC) and Asymmetric Similarity Computation (ASC). In SSC, query is represented in same way as the reference dataset while ASC uses different representations for query and reference dataset. The proposed approach (PCASSB) uses ASC in which query is represented by Integer Query Array (I_A^Q) and Bloom filters are used to represent datasets. Similarity score in SSC is computed by first taking the common set bits of query Bloom filter and i^{th} file's Bloom filter and then Dice coefficient is calculated. The methodology used is demonstrated through an example in Fig. 3.2, where first Bloom filter has seven bits set to *one* and second Bloom filter has eight bits set to *one* and four common positions are set and similarity is computed by using Dice coefficient.

| 0 | 1 | 1 | 0 | 0 | 0 | 0 | 0 | 1 | 0 | 1 | 0 | 0 | 0 | 1 | 0 | 0 | 1 | 0 | 1 |

Bloom filter 1: Seven positions are set 1

| 0 | 1 | 0 | 0 | 1 | 0 | 0 | 0 | 0 | 0 | 1 | 0 | 1 | 0 | 1 | 1 | 0 | 1 | 1 | 0 |

Bloom filter 2: Eight positions are set 1

Common index set as 1 are marked red and their count is 4.

$$\text{Dice coefficient} = \frac{2 \times (\text{Common no. of 1s in Bloom filter 1 and 2})}{(\text{No. of 1s in Bloom filter 1}) + (\text{No. of 1s in Bloom filter 2})}$$

$$= \frac{2 \times 4}{7 + 8} = 0.53$$

Figure 3.2: Bloom filter Similarity through Dice Coefficient

Since Bloom filter generates false positives, some of the common set bits are counted more than once, which need to be subtracted from the common bits C. Thus, Effective Common Bits (ECB) are:

$$ECB = C - (C \times fp) \tag{3.2}$$

here fp is probability of false positives.

In PCASSB, features of each file in the dataset are represented in Bloom filters and query is represented in integer query array. The integer query array stores the indexes generated by the hash functions for each query feature; mapping of query features to integer array is given in Algorithm 3.2. Similarity is computed by checking the indexes stored in array with those in the Bloom filters. Fig. 3.3 depicts the example explaining how hash values of shingles s_1 $\{2, 3, 7, 8, 13, 14, 15\}$ and s_2 $\{2, 4, 5, 9, 10, 11, 18\}$ are represented in Bloom filter BF^Q and integer array ^IQ_A respectively.

In general, Dice coefficient, Jaccard coefficient or Cosine similarity are considered for text analysis in token based similarity search. Dice similarity has been selected for similarity measure in the proposed approach since it has been experimentally verified (Table 3.1) that Dice coefficient is better than the Cosine similarity method and ranking of the document is not affected by considering this method. Query size indicates the

Chapter 3 A Parallel Computational Approach for Similarity Search using Bloom Filters (PCASSB)

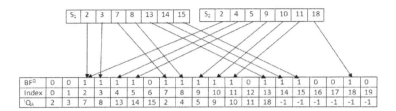

Figure 3.3: Query in Bloom filter and Integer array

Input: A query Q and integer array ^IQ_A.
Output: Indexed values of Q in ^IQ_A
1 Shingles = fileToShingles(Q)
2 **for** $i=0$ to $|Shingles|-1$ **do**
3   **for** $j=0$ to $k-1$ **do**
4        $^IQ_A[i \times k + j] = H_j(Shingles[i])$
5   **end**
6 **end**

Algorithm 3.2: Mapping of Query words into integer array

Table 3.1: Time [ms] required to calculate similarity score by various similarity computing methods

No. of files	Query size	Dice	Jaccard	Cosine
50	20	49	44	52
	50	39	40	40
	100	44	44	47
100	20	83	82	88
	50	83	83	83
	100	104	97	85
200	20	157	154	166
	50	156	156	156
	100	167	178	210
500	20	551	547	536
	50	569	553	572
	100	639	635	630
1,000	20	1,010	1,003	1,035
	50	1,005	977	996
	100	1,178	979	1,276
2,000	20	2,068	2,016	1,968
	50	1,897	1,898	1,921
	100	1,900	1,904	1,919
5,000	20	4,437	4,574	4,598
	50	4,518	4,710	4,751
	100	4,504	4,510	4,524
9,000	20	8,496	9,108	8,572
	50	8,360	8,348	8,844
	100	8,452	8,380	8,438
14,000	20	12,694	12,722	13,052
	50	12,770	12,746	12,797
	100	13,525	13,964	12,912

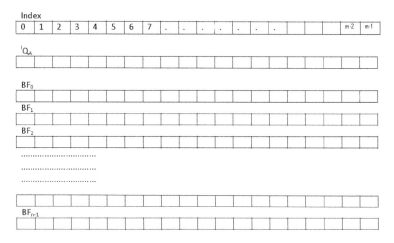

Figure 3.4: Parallel arrangements of Query and Documents

number of shingles generated from user's query. After the mapping of query array (^IQ_A) to GPU memory, a kernel is launched (PCASSB<<<grid(,), block(,)>>>) from CPU with appropriate configuration to start parallel search operation on GPU which compares query (^IQ_A) with reference dataset (BF_i), $\forall i, 1 \geq i \geq n$. In PCASSB, query index values stored in ^IQ_A are checked in Bloom filter BF_i, where data is initially stored. Fig. 3.4 depicts the parallel arrangement for Query and Documents. If all k indexes of a query shingle have value *one* in corresponding BF_i, item is considered as similar and count is incremented by 1. This procedure is repeated for all query items. Similarity score of each document, corresponding to the user's query, is computed based on the final value achieved. Similarly, the similarity score for query ^IQ_A and BF_i $\forall i$ where $1 \leq i \leq |D|$ is computed. The value i for i^{th} Bloom filter BF_i is generated by *fId* computed in Algorithm 3.3 (Line 1). These *fId* values are generated for all thread blocks and processing of file and query is done in parallel on individual thread blocks.

Input: Bloom filter of documents BF_i^D and query array ^IQ_A
Output: Similarity score D_i^{sim}

1. $fId = blockIdx.y \times gridDim.x \times blockDim.z \times blockDim.y \times blockDim.x + blockIdx.x \times blockDim.z \times blockDim.y \times blockDim.x + threadIdx.z \times blockDim.y \times blockDim.x + threadIdx.y \times blockDim.x + threadIdx.x;$
2. $|B_c| = 0$ /*count of common bits*/
3. $|C_s| = 0$ /*count of common items*/
4. $|Q_s| = \dfrac{|^IQ_A|}{k}$ /*Q_s is total number shingles in query and k is number of hash functions*/
5. i= fId **for** $s=0$ to $|Q_s| - 1$ **do**
6. $\quad S_o = s \times k$ /*S_o is Shingle offset*/
7. $\quad$ **for** $f=0$ to k-1 **do**
8. $\quad\quad |B_c| += BF_i^D[^IQ_A[S_o + f]]$
9. $\quad$ **end**
10. $\quad$ **if** $|B_c| = k$ **then**
11. $\quad\quad |C_s| += 1$
12. $\quad$ **end**
13. **end**
14. $|D_i^s|$ = number of shingles in i^{th} document
15. $D_i^{sim} = \dfrac{2 \times |C_s|}{|Q_s| + |D_i^s|}$ /*D_i^{sim} is similarity score of ith document with query*/

Algorithm 3.3: Similarity score computation using PCASSB

3.1.2.3 Ranking

Once the similarity score is computed for all the documents, they are sorted in parallel. Sorting is performed on GPU using odd-even sorting. Sorted similarity score of the documents are transferred back to the CPU memory.

Table 3.2: Bloom filter parameters

Parameter	Description	Values generated	Values considered
f_p	False Positives (Eq. (1.10))	0.01	0.01
n	Number of words	400	600
m	Bloom filter size (Eq. (1.12))	3,834.02	4,096
k	Number of hash functions (Eq. (1.11))	6.7	7

3.2 Experimental Results and Analysis

The effectiveness of the proposed approach has been evaluated by considering varying number of files and query size. Proposed approach has been run on both CPU and GPU. It has been implemented on GPU using CUDA platform for parallel version and serial version is developed using C# programming language.

3.2.1 Dataset

Dataset used to evaluate the proposed approach is publicly available 20Newsgroups [150] dataset. It contains 20 group of news articles with each group containing 1000 documents and 14,000 files have been selected for experimentation, after discarding files which were quite big or small. All documents have been merged into single group to find inter group similarity. At the initial stage, dataset is preprocessed to remove stop words and features are extracted in the form of k-shingles.

3.2.2 Parameter Setting

For n items, performance of the Bloom filter, depends on m, the size of Bloom filter and k, the number of hash functions. The optimal selection of these two parameters are derived from Eq.1.10, 1.11 and 1.12. Since most of the documents considered in the dataset are in the range of 200 to 600 words, the size of Bloom filter is selected as 4096 and seven hash functions have been used for hashing the shingles of the documents. Table 3.2 provides the values generated experimentally and values considered for parameters n, m and k corresponding to various parameters considered in Bloom filter for experimental purpose.

3.2.3 System Configuration

Serial tasks are processed by CPU and parallel tasks are performed on GPU. Fedora 21.0 and CUDA 7.5 with GPU NVIDIA GeForce GTX 680 is used with 1,024 threads. GPU kernel is called with grid and block which generates the threads; based on the thread id, file is processed by the respective thread.

3.2.4 Experimental Results

The similarity score of documents is generated against query and compared with the baseline method. Table 3.3 represents the data for top 15 documents while the graphs depict the results for 50 documents.

- Initially, documents are sorted in ascending and descending order based on similarity scores computed by baseline (Dice coefficient) method.

- Next, similarity scores of documents are compared with the proposed approach (PCASSB). Similarity score ranges between 0 to 1; $Similarity_{Score} = 1$ indicates identical documents and $Similarity_{Score} = 0$ indicates completely dissimilar documents.

- Finally, the similarity scores for documents are analysed in terms of accuracy. Accuracy is computed as $(1 - Error_{PCASSB})$ and error is absolute difference between the results generated by Dice coefficient and PCASSB.

$$Error_{PCASSB} = |Similarity_{DC} - Similarity_{PCASSB}| \tag{3.3}$$

$$Accuracy(\%) = Round(((1 - Error_{PCASSB}) \times 100), 4) \tag{3.4}$$

3.2.4.1 Similarity Score of Documents Corresponding to Query

Similarity and accuracy of most similar files (arranged in decreasing order) corresponding to user's query are depicted in Table 3.3. Table 3.4 provides similarity and accu-

Table 3.3: Similarity and accuracy of most similar files

Files with maximum similarity score (in decreasing order)	Similarity>=0.12		
	Dice Similarity	PCASSB (Proposed) Similarity	Accuracy
1	1	1	100.0000
2	0.1935	0.1803	98.6752
3	0.1538	0.1406	98.6754
4	0.1497	0.1379	98.8240
5	0.1401	0.1290	98.8873
6	0.1389	0.1268	98.7911
7	0.1387	0.1287	98.9972
8	0.1379	0.1228	98.4869
9	0.1375	0.1266	98.9100
10	0.1375	0.1266	98.9100
11	0.1351	0.1233	98.8165
12	0.1304	0.1209	99.0465
13	0.1299	0.1184	98.8530
14	0.1287	0.1183	98.9645
15	0.1282	0.1169	98.8695

Table 3.4: Similarity and accuracy of dissimilar files

Files with minimum similarity score (in increasing order)	Similarity<0.03		
	Dice Similarity	PCASSB (Proposed) Similarity	Accuracy
1	0.0081	0.0162	99.1875
2	0.0081	0.0135	99.4586
3	0.0081	0.0108	99.7308
4	0.0081	0.0270	98.1119
5	0.0081	0.0108	99.7319
6	0.0081	0.0189	98.9230
7	0.0081	0.0163	99.1830
8	0.0081	0.0136	99.4541
9	0.0082	0.0136	99.4552
10	0.0082	0.0136	99.4563
11	0.0082	0.0162	99.1963
12	0.0082	0.0163	99.1874
13	0.0082	0.0218	98.6374
14	0.0082	0.0082	99.9974
15	0.0082	0.0245	98.3686

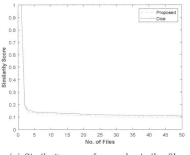 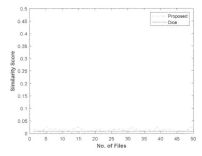

(a) Similarity score for nearly similar files   (b) Similarity score for least similar files

Figure 3.5: Similarity score computed by Dice and PCASSB for nearly and least similar files.

racy of dissimilar files (arranged in increasing order) against user's query. In Table 3.3 and 3.4, similarity computed by Dice coefficient is assumed as precise as it is computed based on the intersection of query features and documents features. Accuracy achieved by PCASSB is same as achieved in the approach proposed by Iacob et al. [19] but PCASSB takes less time. Accuracy of PCASSB have been graphically demonstrated in Fig. 3.5(a). Generally Bloom filters based similarity computation do not provide accurate results when queried items are not present in reference dataset i.e. they have very low similarity score. Results achieved clearly indicate that similarity computed by baseline method and PCASSB are identical, indicating that there is no loss of accuracy by using the proposed scheme. The reason behind high false positive probability is that Bloom filter uses hash functions to set bits in bit array and generated hash values are always in that range 0 to m-1, where m is the size of Bloom filter. At the time of query, although the item is not present in table, indexes generated by hash functions will be in same range i.e. 0 to m-1, thus they could be matched. The proposed approach is robust in such cases as similarity is acknowledged only when all bits are set high.

Fig. 3.5(a) and 3.5(b) depict the similarity scores computed by the PCASSB and baseline method when similarity between query and reference dataset are high and low

Chapter 3 A Parallel Computational Approach for Similarity Search using Bloom Filters (PCASSB)

Table 3.5: Query search time [ms] on CPU and GPU by Dice and PCASSB

Method→	CPU		GPU
No. of files ↓	Dice	PCASSB	PCASSB
5,000	7,320	49	7
9,000	14,352	91	13
14,000	22,302	137	22

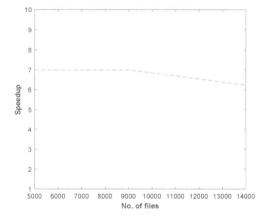

Figure 3.6: Speedup of PCASSB on GPU

respectively. As seen from Table 3.3, PCASSB gives 98% accuracy in majority of the cases indicating that it performs efficiently in terms of accuracy and speedup.

3.2.4.2 Query Search Time in CPU and GPU

Table 3.5 shows the query search time of Dice and PCASSB while running on CPU and GPU. Computation time is drastically reduced when the proposed approach is implemented on GPU and the speedup achieved is demonstrated in Fig. 3.6. Speedup for GPU does not increases once the number of files and the number of processing units available in GPU are equal. Further, PCASSB is adaptive to query size as it takes less time if query size is small. Fig. 3.7 and 3.8 depict Query search time *vs.* No. of Files on CPU and GPU with varying query size.

Chapter 3 A Parallel Computational Approach for Similarity Search using Bloom Filters (PCASSB)

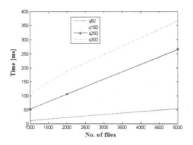

Figure 3.7: Query search time *vs.* No. of files on CPU with varying query size

Figure 3.8: Query search time *vs.* No. of files on GPU with varying query size

Table 3.6: CPU search time [ms] for various state-of-the-art approaches

No. of files	Query Size	Randall et al. [29]	Jain et al. [39]	Iacob et al. [19]	PCASSB (Proposed)
50	20	4	5	1	1
	50	4	4	1	1
	100	4	5	1	1
100	20	7	9	1	1
	50	8	9	1	1
	100	8	10	1	1
200	20	15	18	1	1
	50	16	19	1	1
	100	16	19	3	3
500	20	39	47	2	2
	50	40	47	4	4
	100	40	49	9	8
1,000	20	77	97	4	4
	50	80	98	9	9
	100	81	101	18	18
2,000	20	156	206	8	8
	50	161	210	19	19
	100	165	216	39	38
5,000	20	442	527	21	21
	50	401	515	48	48
	100	436	606	98	98
9,000	20	701	1,069	38	38
	50	723	942	109	88
	100	803	1,181	201	190
14,000	20	1,112	1,446	59	48
	50	1,127	1,511	136	120
	100	1,397	1,852	317	310

Table 3.6 shows the execution time for search operation on the CPU corresponding to the query where test is performed for different number of files with varying query size and search time is shown for various state-of-the-art methods and the proposed approach. From Table 3.6 it is observed that the search time for Iacob *et al.* [19] approach and PCASSB is almost same and better than the other approaches.

Table 3.7: GPU execution time [ms] for query search and ranking of documents

Methods		PCASSB (Proposed)			Iacob *et al.* [19]		
No. of files	Query size	Search time	Ranking time	Total time	Search time	Ranking time	Total time
50	20	0.05	0.23	0.28	0.06	0.01	0.07
	50	0.10	0.32	0.42	0.11	0.01	0.12
	100	0.18	0.20	0.39	0.19	0.01	0.19
100	20	0.08	0.42	0.50	0.08	0.02	0.10
	50	0.16	0.47	0.64	0.16	0.02	0.18
	100	0.30	0.43	0.73	0.30	0.02	0.32
200	20	0.09	0.81	0.90	0.10	0.09	0.19
	50	0.19	0.80	0.99	0.19	0.05	0.24
	100	0.36	0.83	1.19	0.37	0.05	0.42
500	20	0.12	1.91	2.03	0.11	0.55	0.66
	50	0.24	1.90	2.14	0.24	0.30	0.54
	100	0.46	1.90	2.36	0.46	0.30	0.76
1,000	20	0.17	3.95	4.12	0.17	2.12	2.28
	50	0.37	3.95	4.31	0.36	1.02	1.38
	100	0.68	4.09	4.77	0.68	0.97	1.65
2,000	20	0.33	7.90	8.23	0.32	7.89	8.21
	50	0.69	8.10	8.79	0.74	4.09	4.83
	100	1.32	7.98	9.30	1.32	3.68	5.00
5,000	20	0.76	2.54	3.30	0.81	43.92	44.74
	50	1.84	2.54	4.39	1.87	21.90	23.77
	100	3.62	2.57	6.19	3.64	17.66	21.30
9,000	20	1.53	4.64	6.17	1.64	129.07	130.71
	50	3.80	4.57	8.36	3.80	63.22	67.02
	100	7.21	4.28	11.49	7.23	57.42	64.65
14,000	20	0.06	7.10	7.16	2.17	300.92	303.08
	50	0.11	6.24	6.35	4.89	148.63	153.51
	100	0.19	7.07	7.27	9.41	135.83	145.24

In Table 3.7 execution time for PCASSB and Iacob *et al.* [19] approach is demonstrated for varying query size and number of files and it is observed that the search time for the proposed approach and Iacob *et al.* approach is almost similar but ranking of the retrieved documents is better in PCASSB due to parallel sorting through GPU. It is observed from the Table 3.7 that in some of the cases, when number of files are less, Iacob *et al.* approach performs better, due to memory transfer process involve in GPU based approach but when the number of files are more then 5,000, PCASSB outperforms Iacob *et al.* approach significantly. The main advantage of PCASSB is that it runs in parallel for both searching and ranking operation, which are required to be online and fast as one need to respond to user's query instantly.

Space complexity of PCASSB: PCASSB uses Bloom filter for document representation, which takes only bit array to represent the document. Lets consider a document consisting of 400 words with each word having five character where each character is represented by 8 bits.

Case I: Memory required to represent the document: $400 \times 5 \times 8 = 16,000$ bits

Case II: Memory required to represent the document using Bloom filter: 4,096 (Bloom size generated using Eq. 1.12) Thus, memory required in Case II is 25% of that required in Case I.

The main contributions of this chapter are:

- Hash keys of query words are stored in an integer query array instead of Bloom filter. Integer query array representation of query supports index based search.

- Similarity matching of query with documents is performed by checking query indexes in Bloom filters of documents. It has been experimentally proved that index based matching technique improves the accuracy.

- Proposed approach performs parallel searching and sorting using GPU which helps in reducing the execution time drastically.

Next chapter discusses the similarity search approaches for images.

Chapter 4

Similarity Search Approaches for Image Datasets

In this chapter, two similarity search approaches for image datasets have been proposed. The proposed approaches are named as "An efficient Bi-layer Content Based Image Retrieval approach" (BiCBIR) and "Efficient Layer-wise Feature Incremental Approach for Content Based Image Retrieval System" (FiCBIR)

4.1 Introduction

In CBIR systems, images having visual contents similar to the corresponding query image are retrieved from the image dataset. Generally CBIR systems work in two stages: In the first stage, features of the dataset images are extracted and stored in feature vectors. In the second stage, query image features are compared with images in the dataset. A general overview of CBIR system is given in Fig. 4.1. Generally, CBIR systems use multiple image features to represent an image. Thus the query image needs to be compared with all the images of the dataset for all the features, *i.e.*, color, texture and shape. When the image dataset is large, retrieval of images similar to the query image requires large computational time. Further, in the image dataset, images relevant to query image are very few, hence, it is important to prune those irrelevant images. To minimize computational cost, image retrieval systems have been

Chapter 4 Similarity Search Approaches for Image Datasets   57

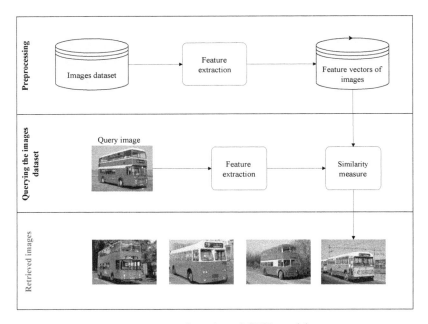

Figure 4.1: Overview of CBIR model

introduced which uses layered approach. In this work two image retrieval approaches are proposed named as "An efficient Bi-layer Content Based Image Retrieval approach" (BiCBIR) and "Efficient Layer-wise Feature Incremental Approach for Content Based Image Retrieval System" (FiCBIR). The proposed approaches consist of two modules: feature extraction process and retrieval process. Feature extraction process is same for both the approaches. Retrieval process in BiCBIR is further divided into two layers and in FiCBIR it is performed in three layers. Both approaches use three image features namely color, texture and shape. Feature extraction process is discussed in Section 4.2. The similarity computation methods used in the proposed approaches are provided in Section 4.3. The proposed approaches BiCBIR and FiCBIR are discussed in Section 4.4 and 4.5 respectively.

4.2 Image Feature Extraction

For a image dataset $I_{DB} = \{I_1, I_2, I_3, \ldots, I_n\}$ consisting of n images, features extracted for a particular image I are: color I^c, texture I^t and shape I^s along with a fixed size feature vector (Fig. 4.2).

4.2.1 Color Feature Extraction

Color features are extracted by using histogram of quantized values of color in Hue (H), Saturation (S) and Value (V) color space. Since HSV color space is more robust to human perception as compared to RGB color space [151], RGB images are converted to HSV color space and then uniform quantization is applied (Eq.(4.1)). Feature vectors are generated by considering the values of H=9, S=3 and V=3 to form the feature vector of size 81 bin. Representation of color feature vector of an image is given in Eq. 4.2.

$$H = \begin{cases} 0 & h \in [1, 40] \\ 1 & h \in [41, 80] \\ 2 & h \in [81, 120] \\ 3 & h \in [121, 160] \\ 4 & h \in [161, 200] \\ 5 & h \in [201, 240] \\ 6 & h \in [241, 280] \\ 7 & h \in [281, 320] \\ 8 & h \in [321, 360] \end{cases} \quad S = \begin{cases} 0 & s \in [0.00, 0.30] \\ 1 & s \in [0.31, 0.70] \\ 2 & s \in [0.71, 1.00] \end{cases} \quad V = \begin{cases} 0 & v \in [0.00, 0.30] \\ 1 & v \in [0.31, 0.70] \\ 2 & v \in [0.71, 1.00] \end{cases} \quad (4.1)$$

$$IF^c = \{IF_1^c, IF_2^c, IF_3^c, \ldots, IF_{cn}^c\} \quad (4.2)$$

4.2.2 Texture Feature Extraction

Gabor filter [152], introduced by Gabor in 1946, is one of the widely used filter for texture feature extraction. It is a Gaussian function modulated by complex sinusoidal of frequency and orientation [153]. In this work, texture features of an image are extracted by using five scales (s) and six orientations (o). The usage of multiple s and o makes the features rotation and scaling invariant on texture feature space. Different combination of s and o form the feature vector for texture space of length sixty, where first thirty values represent mean and next thirty values represent standard deviation of texture descriptors. To construct texture feature vector, a two dimensional Gabor function $G_f(x, y)$ and its Fourier transform $FT(u, v)$ is considered; represented as:

$$GF(x,y) = \left(\frac{1}{2\pi\sigma_x\sigma_y}\right) \exp\left(-\frac{1}{2}\left(\frac{x^2}{\sigma_x^2} + \frac{y^2}{\sigma_y^2}\right) + 2\pi j C_f x\right) \tag{4.3}$$

$$FT(u,v) = \exp\left(\frac{1}{2}\left[\frac{(u-C_f)^2}{\sigma_u^2} + \frac{v^2}{\sigma_v^2}\right]\right) \tag{4.4}$$

where $\sigma_u = \dfrac{1}{2\pi\sigma_x}$, $\sigma_v = \dfrac{1}{2\pi\sigma_y}$ and C_f is a constant representing the center frequency of the filter bank having the highest frequency. A Gabor filter bank having a number of bandpass filters, with varying center frequencies, bandwidths and orientations are controlled by the parameters of Gabor wavelets. An input image, $I(x, y)$ when filtered by the set of Gabor wavelets $G_f(x, y)$, is given as:

$$R_{mn}(x,y) = \int I(x,y) GF^*_{mn}(x - x_1, y - y_1) dx_1 dy_1 \tag{4.5}$$

where $RF_{mn}(x,y)$ is the filter response at the spatial location (x, y); m = 1, 2, ..., s is the number of scales and n = 1, 2, ..., o is the number of orientations. It is assumed that local image regions are spatially homogeneous and mean and standard deviation of the magnitude of the filter responses are used to represent the region for matching purposes:

$$\mu_{mn} = \int\int |RF_{mn}(x,y)| \, dx dy \tag{4.6}$$

$$\sigma_{mn} = \sqrt{\int\int(\mid RF_{mn}(x,y)\mid -\mu_{mn})^2 dxdy} \qquad (4.7)$$

A feature vector is constructed using μ_{mn} and σ_{mn} as feature components and texture feature descriptor are given as:

$$IF^t = \{IF_{11}^m, IF_{12}^m, \ldots, IF^m s \times o, IF_{11}^{sd}, IF_{12}^{sd}, \ldots, IF_{s\times o}^{sd}\} \qquad (4.8)$$

4.2.3 Shape Feature Extraction

Shape features are extracted using Zernike Moments (ZM) [154]. ZM are rotation invariant and use zernike polynomials to form feature vector to represent an image based on shape features. ZMs are defined as the projections of f(x,y) on a class of polynomials, called Zernike polynomials. The complete set of Zernike polynomials is defined as:

$$V_{nm}(\rho,\theta) = R_{nm}(\rho)e^{jm\theta} \qquad (4.9)$$

where $R_{nm}(\rho)$ are real-valued radial polynomials and Eq. 4.10 gives the orthogonal property of $V_{nm}^*(\rho,\theta)$:

$$\int\int_{\substack{0\leq\rho\leq 1 \\ 0\leq\theta\leq 2\pi}} V_{nm}^*(\rho,\theta)V_{n'm'}(\rho,\theta)\rho d\rho d\theta = \frac{\pi}{n+1}\delta_{nn'}\delta_{mm'} \qquad (4.10)$$

where $*$ denotes the complex conjugate and $\delta_{mm'}$ is

$$\delta_{nn'} = \begin{cases} 1, & n = n' \\ 0, & otherwise. \end{cases} \qquad (4.11)$$

ZM of order n with repetition m for a continuous image function $f(x,y)$ over a unit disk is:

$$A_{nm} = \frac{n+1}{\pi}\int\int_{unit\ disk} V_{nm}^*(x,y)f(x,y)dxdy. \qquad (4.12)$$

Chapter 4 Similarity Search Approaches for Image Datasets

For digital images, the integrals can be replaced by summations

$$A_{nm} = \frac{n+1}{\pi} \sum_x \sum_y f(x,y) V_{nm}^*(x,y), \qquad x^2 + y^2 \leq 1 \qquad (4.13)$$

In this work, twenty one initial zernike moments are used to represent the images; shape feature vector is represented in Eq. 4.14.

$$IF^s = \{IF_1^s, IF_2^s, IF_3^s, \ldots, IF_{sn}^s\} \qquad (4.14)$$

Input:
I_{DB}: Image datasets
$C_{H=9}$: Hue of HSV color space for an image
$C_{S=3}$: Saturation of HSV color space for an image
$C_{V=3}$: Value of HSV color space for an image
$T_{S=5}$: Scales of image for texture features
$T_{O=6}$: Orientations of image for texture features
$S_{M=5}$: Repetition of moments of an image for shape features
Output:
F_{DB}: Features database of I_{DB} which includes following vectors
C_f: Color feature vectors having dimensions 81 (9 × 3 × 3)
T_f: Texture feature vectors having dimensions 60 (5 × 6 + 5 × 6)
S_f: Shape feature vectors having dimensions 21
1 imgCount=size(I_{DB})
2 **for** $i=1$ to imgCount **do**
3 $\quad C_f[i] = \text{colorFeature}(I_{DB}[i], C_H, C_S, C_V)$
4 $\quad T_f[i] = \text{textureFeature}(I_{DB}[i], T_S, T_O)$
5 $\quad S_f[i] = \text{shapeFeature}(I_{DB}[i], M)$
6 $\quad I_{imagePath} = I_{DB}[i]$
7 $\quad F_{DB}[i] = [C_f[i] T_f[i] S_f[i]]$
8 **end**
9 return F_{DB}

Algorithm 4.1: Image features extraction

For a image I, separate feature vector is created for color features IF^c, texture features IF^t and shape features IF^s.

Table 4.1: Image feature type and vector length

Type	Vector length	Description
Color	81	Color features are extracted by using histogram on HSV color space
Texture	60	Texture features are obtained from Gabor filter with scales and six orientations
Shape	21	Shape features are generated obtained from zernike moments

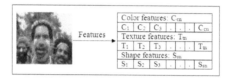

Figure 4.2: Vector representation of extracted image features

Table 4.2: Structure of image feature vectors in database

Image Id	Features													
	Color					Texture					Shape				
Img_1	C_1	C_2	.	.	.	C_{cn}	T_1	T_2	.	.	.	T_{tn}	S_1	S_2	.	.	.	S_{sn}
Img_2															
...				...					...					...
Img_n				...					...					...

4.3 Similarity Computation

To compute similarity between query image, Q_i, and the data set, I_{DH}, similarity functions are required. In this work, color similarity (C_{ss}) is computed by using cosine distance (Eq. (4.15)). Similarity of texture (T_{ss}) and shape (S_{ss}) features is computed by using Euclidean distance (Eq. 4.16)).

$$Cosine\ Distance\ (CD) = \frac{\langle I^f \cdot Q^f \rangle}{\parallel I^f \parallel \parallel Q^f \parallel} \qquad (4.15)$$

$$Euclidean\ Distance\ (ED) = \sum_{i=1}^{|f|} \sqrt{(I^f - Q^f)^2} \qquad (4.16)$$

$$C_{ss} = Sim(Q^c, IF_i^c, CD) \qquad (4.17)$$

$$T_{ss} = Sim(Q^t, IF_i^t, ED) \qquad (4.18)$$

$$S_{ss} = Sim(Q^s, IF_i^s, ED) \qquad (4.19)$$

Input:

Q^f: Feature vector query image for f feature type, which can be color, texture or shape

I^f: Feature vector of an image from dataset for f feature

DM: Distance measure function, which can be cosine or euclidean.

Output:

SS: Similarity score between Q^f and I^f by using DM

1 **if** $f =$ 'Shape' or $f =$ 'Texture' **then**
2 $\quad SS = \sum_{i=1}^{|f|} \sqrt{(I^f - Q^f)^2}$
3 **else**
4 $\quad SS = \frac{\langle I^f \cdot Q^f \rangle}{\|I^f\| \|Q^f\|}$
5 *Return SS*

Algorithm 4.2: Similarity computation

4.4 An Efficient bi-layer CBIR approach (BiCBIR)

BiCBIR approach consists into two modules. In the first module, image features of the dataset images are extracted in the form of color, texture and shape (Section 4.2). In the second module image retrieval task is performed, which is further divided into two layers (Section 4.4.1). The overview of the proposed approach is demonstrated in Fig. 4.3.

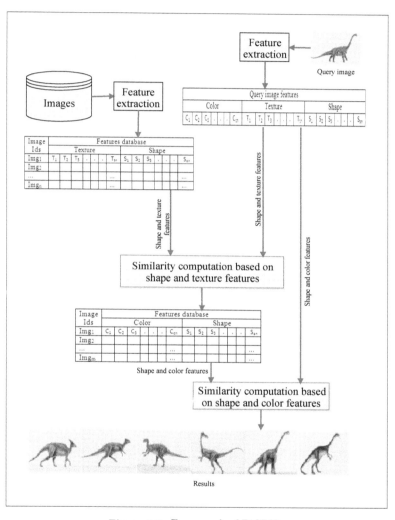

Figure 4.3: Framework of BiCBIR.

4.4.1 Retrieval of Images Similar to the Query Image in BiCBIR

Features of the query image, Q_i, are extracted and a separate feature vector is formed for each feature type, *i.e.*, color, texture and shape. Features vectors for query images are represented in Eq. 4.20. Images which are visually similar to Q_i are retrieved by using a two layer approach given in Algorithm 4.3.

$$Q^c = \{Q_1^c, Q_2^c, Q_3^c, \ldots, Q_{cn}^c\}$$
$$Q^t = \{Q_1^t, Q_2^t, Q_3^t, \ldots, Q_{tn}^t\}$$
$$Q^s = \{Q_1^s, Q_2^s, Q_3^s, \ldots, Q_{sn}^s\} \tag{4.20}$$

Table 4.3: CBIR variants based on the number of layer(s) and feature(s)

Method	Feature	Category
C	Color	In this category, different methods, compute the similarity in single layer and on single feature space in C, T and S retrieval methods whereas $CTS1$ combines color, texture and shape features.
T	Texture	
S	Shape	
$CTS1$	Color + Texture + Shape	
TCCS	Layer1: Color + Texture and Layer2: Color + Shape	This category contains the image retrieval methods which compute the similarity in two layers. First layer computes the similarity of query image with all N images in the dataset while second layer computes similarity of only M images having similarity score more than the rest of the images where M is 20% of N.
CTTS	Layer1: Texture + Color and Layer2: Texture + Shape	
CSST	Layer1: Shape + Color and Layer2: Shape + Texture	
SCCT	Layer1: Color + Shape and Layer2: Color + Texture	
STTC	Layer1: Texture + Shape and Layer2: Texture + Color	
TSSC	Layer1: Shape + Texture and Layer2: Shape + Color	
CTS	Layer1: Color, Layer2: Texture and Layer3: Shape	Methods belonging to this category comprise of three layers. First layer compares all the N images with query image and returns M_1 images to second layer, second layer compares only M_1 images and returns M_2 images to third layer. Third layer compares M_2 images and finally returns F images to the end user, where $N \gg M_1 > M_2 > F$ (M_1 is 10% of N, M_2 is 20% of N and F is 20).
CST	Layer1: Color, Layer2: Shape and Layer3: Texture	
TCS	Layer1: Texture, Layer2: Color and Layer3: Shape	
TSC	Layer1: Texture, Layer2: Shape and Layer3: Color	
STC	Layer1: Shape, Layer2: Texture and Layer3: Color	
SCT	Layer1: Shape, Layer2: Color and Layer3: Texture	

In the first layer, two features namely shape and texture are used to compute the similarity of Q_i and I_{DB}. The indexes of M most similar images, produced by pruning the non-relevant images based on similarity computed from first layer, named as I_{DBM},

66   *Chapter 4 Similarity Search Approaches for Image Datasets*

serve as input to the second layer. In second layer, shape and color features of Q_i and I_{DBM} are matched and the indexes of F most similar images, named as I_{DBOut}, are retrieved as output.

Input:
Q: Query image
F_{DB}: Features database of I_{DB} which includes following vectors
RI_{L1}: Total number of images to be retreived from layer 1.
Output:
Q^C: Color feature vector of query image
Q^T: Texture feature vector of query image
Q^S: Shape feature vector of query image
$Img_{indexes}$: indexes of relevent images after pruning of non-relevent images

1   $Q^C = \text{colorFeature}(Q, C_H, C_S, C_V)$
2   $Q^T = \text{textureFeature}(Q, T_S, T_O)$
3   $Q^S = \text{shapeFeature}(Q, M)$
4   **for** *i=1 to n* **do**
5      $SS_{L1}(i, 1) = \text{imgIndex}(i)$
6      $SS_{L1}(i, 2) = \dfrac{sim(Q^S, F_{DB}^S[i]) + sim(Q^T, F_{DB}^T[i])}{2}$
7   **end**
8   $SM_{L1} = \text{Sort}(SS_{L1}, \text{Ascending})$
9   $RI_{DB} = SM_{L1}(1 : RI_{L1})$
10   **for** *i=1 to RI_{L1}* **do**
11      $SS_{L2}(i, 1) = SM_{L1}[i]$
12      $SS_{L2}(i, 2) =$
13      $\dfrac{sim(Q^S, F_{DB}^S[RI_{DB}[i]]) + sim(Q^C, F_{DB}^C[RI_{DB}[i]])}{2}$
14   **end**
15   $SM_{L2} = \text{Sort}(SS_{L2}, \text{Ascending})$
16   $Return\ SM_{L2}(1 : F)$

Algorithm 4.3: Retrieval process of BiCBIR

As seen in Algorithm 4.3, both layers use one common feature, shape, which partially preserves the similarity computed in first layer to the second layer. The selection of features sequence in first and second layer is based on the experimental analysis. Experiments have been performed for all possible sequences and the sequence which generates the best retrieval rate is considered in the proposed approach. The idea of having a common feature in two layers makes the proposed approach robust.

4.5 Efficient layer-wise Feature incremental approach for CBIR system (FiCBIR)

FiCBIR works in two modules: feature extraction and image retrieval. In this work three primitive image features namely color, texture and shape are considered for image representation. The retrieval process takes place in three layers which uses single feature in first layer, combination of two features in second layer and all three features in final layer for measuring the similarity between query image and target dataset images. A block diagram in Fig. 4.4 provides an overview of FiCBIR. Table 4.4 shows the layer wise feature merging for similarity measure. The details of first module, *i.e.*, image feature extraction have been discussed in section 4.2 and second module, *i.e.*, image retrieval is discussed in the section 4.5.1.

Table 4.4: Layer wise incremental usage of feature selection

Layers	Features
Layer 1 (L_1)	F_1
Layer 2 (L_2)	$F_1 + F_2$
Layer 3 (L_3)	$F_1 + F_2 + F_3$

4.5.1 Retrieval of Images Similar to the Query Image in FiCBIR

In general, an image dataset contains huge number of images but very few images are relevant for a particular query image. The search complexity of CBIR system depends on two factors: the number of images in the dataset and the size of features used for image representation. To avoid exhaustive search process for all the images in full feature space, a 3-layer image retrieval approach has been proposed. The proposed approach uses only single type of feature F_1 for similarity computation at the first layer and all the N images are compared and L_1 most similar images are returned to the second layer. In the second layer, similarity between query image and L_1 images, retrieved from first layer, is computed by combining F_1 and F_2 feature space. Second

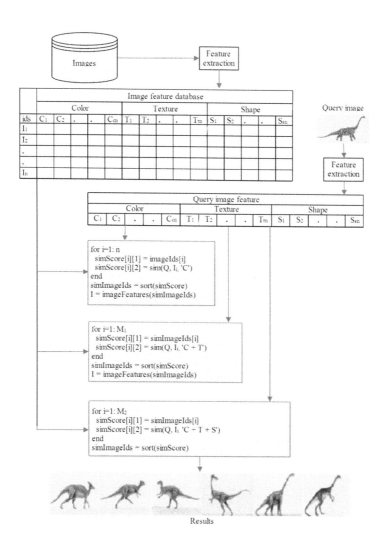

Figure 4.4: Framework of FiCBIR.

Chapter 4 Similarity Search Approaches for Image Datasets

layer returns L_2 images which are most relevant to the query. Final layer combines F_1, F_2 and F_3 features and similarity between query image and dataset images is computed. The final layer returns F images which are most similar to the query image.

Table 4.5 provides the description of image retrieval methods (M1 To M13) based on feature(s) considered at individual layers L_1, L_2 and L_3. M1 method consider all three feature and single layer. Methods M2 to M7 consider three layers where single feature is considered at each layer. Method M8 to M13 consider single feature at layer 1, two features at layer 2 and all three feature at layer 3. The proposed approach has been tested with six variants of possible feature sequences at different layers (M8 to M13 in Table 4.5). In this module, when the query is generated, all three types of

Table 4.5: Methods categorization based on retrieval layers and features considered in the respective layer(s)

Methods	Description
$M1$	Uses combination of color, texture and shape feature to compute the similarity.
$M2$	L_1: Color, L_2: Texture, L_3: Shape
$M3$	L_1: Color, L_2: Shape, L_3: Texture
$M4$	L_1: Texture, L_2: Color, L_3: Shape
$M5$	L_1: Texture, L_2: Shape, L_3: Color
$M6$	L_1: Shape, L_2: Color, L_3: Texture
$M7$	L_1: Shape, L_2: Texture, L_3: Color
$M8$	L_1: Color, L_2: Color + Texture, L_3: Color + Texture + Shape
$M9$	L_1: Color, L_2: Color + Texture, L_3: Color + Texture + Shape
$M10$	L_1: Texture, L_2: Texture + Color, L_3: Color + Texture + Shape
$M11$	L_1: Texture, L_2: Texture + Shape, L_3: Color + Texture + Shape
$M12$	L_1: Shape, L_2: Shape + Color, L_3: Color + Texture + Shape
$M13$	L_1: Shape, L_2: Shape + Texture, L_3: Color + Texture + Shape

features are extracted in the same way as reference dataset. Searching of images is performed in three layers (Algorithm 4.4). The selected sequence of feature types is: $C \to (C + T) \to (C + T + S)$; this sequence is selected since it has best retrieval performance among all possible layer-wise combinations of the feature spaces. The selected sequence *i.e.* $(C \to (C + T) \to (C + T + S))$ of CBIR method M8 (Table 5.4 to Table 5.7) outperforms all the other methods considered for experimentation.

Input:
Q: Query image
F_{DB}: Feature database
Parameters for color, texture and shape features
Param.H = Hue
Param.S = Saturation
Param.V = Value
Param.s = Scale
Param.o = Orientation
Param.m = Order of zernike moments
Output:
$RetImg$: F most similar images to query image

1. Q_c = FE(Q, Param, C)
2. Q_t = FE(Q, Param, T)
3. Q_s = FE(Q, Param, S)
4. **for** $i=1$ to n **do**
5. $SS_{L1}(i,1)$ = imgIndex(i)
6. $SS_{L1}(i,2) = sim(Q^c, F^c_{DB}[i])$
7. **end**
8. SM_{L1} = Sort(SS_{L1}, Ascending)
9. $RI_{DB} = SM_{L1}(1 : RI_{L2})$
10. **for** $i=1$ to RI_{L1} **do**
11. $SS_{L2}(i,1) = SM_{L1}[i]$
12. $SS_{L2}(i,2) = \dfrac{sim(Q^c, F^c_{DB}[i]) + sim(Q^t, F^t_{DB}[i])}{2}$
13. **end**
14. SM_{L2} = Sort(SS_{L2}, Ascending)
15. $RI_{DB} = SM_{L2}(1 : RI_{L3})$
16. **for** $i=1$ to RI_{L3} **do**
17. $SS_{L3}(i,1) = SM_{L2}[i]$
18. $SS_{L3}(i,2) =$
19. $\dfrac{sim(Q^c, F^c_{DB}[RI_{DB}[i]]) + sim(Q^t, F^t_{DB}[RI_{DB}[i]]) + sim(Q^s, F^s_{DB}[RI_{DB}[i]])}{3}$
20. **end**
21. SM_{L3} = Sort(SS_{L2}, Ascending)
22. $RetImg = SM_{L3}(1 : F)$
23. Return $RetImg$

Algorithm 4.4: Retrieval process of FiCBIR

Chapter 4 Similarity Search Approaches for Image Datasets   **71**

The similarity between query image and dataset images is computed through Algorithm 4.2. Similarity of images is based on distance: if two images have large distance, their similarity is quite low and if two images have small distance then their similarity is high. The range of similarity score lies between 0 and 1.

This chapter discussed the proposed (BiCBIR and FiCBIR) image retrieval techniques using CBIR approach. Chapter 5 provides the implementation details and experimental results of both approaches.

Chapter 5

Implementation Details and Experimental Results

Implementation details of the proposed approaches (BiCBIR and FiCBIR) along with the results of the variants of CBIR based on features and layers is discussed in this chapter.

5.1 Implementation Details

5.1.1 System Configuration

The proposed approaches have been developed and tested on Matlab 2017b software. The hardware configuration of the system used for this work are: Xenon(R) 2.60 GHz processor with 8GB of RAM and Windows 8.1 Pro.

5.1.2 Datasets

BiCBIR has been tested on Wang [155] and GHIM-10k [156] datasets whereas FiCBIR has been tested on four datasets.

i) Wang [155] dataset contains 1000 images of ten categories.

ii) GHIM-10k [156] dataset contains 10000 images of 20 categories with 500 images

Chapter 5 Implementation Details and Experimental Results 73

in each category.

iii) COREL-10k [157] dataset contains 10000 images of 100 categories and each category has 100 images.

iv) Oliva [158] dataset contains 2688 images of eight categories and each category contains different number of images.

5.1.3 Evaluation Parameters

Performance of the proposed approaches have been evaluated on the basis of *precision* (Pr), *recall* (Re) and *f-score* (Fs) @20. The evaluation parameters are given in Eq. (5.1), Eq. (5.2) and Eq. (5.3), respectively.

$$Pr = \frac{|I(Ret) \cap I(Rel)|}{|I(Ret)|} \tag{5.1}$$

$$Re = \frac{|I(Ret) \cap I(Rel)|}{|I(Rel)|} \tag{5.2}$$

$$Fs = \frac{2 \times Pr \times Re}{Pr + Re} \tag{5.3}$$

here I(Ret) are retrieved images and I(Rel) are relevant images.

5.2 Experimental Results of BiCBIR

Results are obtained on the basis of precision, recall and f-score. The experimental results are provided in two subsections, 5.2.1 and 5.2.3. Section 5.2.1 discusses results for sixteen variants of CBIR based on type of features, number of features, sequence of features and number of layers used for image retrieval. In section 5.2.3 the best method among all the methods considered in Section 5.2.1 is selected and compared with other state-of-the-art methods. The bar graphs have been generated for each category of CBIR model, evaluation parameters and datasets. Results shown in tables (Table 5.1 and Table 5.2) include all sixteen variants of CBIR.

5.2.1 Variants of CBIR

The experiments are performed on sixteen variants of image retrieval approach which are grouped into three categories: a) Single layer CBIR model, b) Bi-layer CBIR model and c) Tri-layer CBIR model. These variants are tested on two datasets namely COREL [159] and GHIM [160]. Performance of the single layer CBIR approaches is demonstrated in Fig. 5.1(a), Fig. 5.1(b) and Fig. 5.1(c), respectively for COREL dataset. Fig. 5.2(a), Fig. 5.2(b) and Fig. 5.2(c) show the precision, recall and f-score for GHIM dataset. It has been observed from the Fig. 5.1(a) and Fig. 5.2(a) that in both COREL and GHIM dataset, in comparison to single feature, better results are produced when all three features are combined. Further, the results vary for different datasets when single feature is considered; for COREL dataset shape feature performs well while texture feature provides better retrieval results for GHIM dataset.

The retrieval results of two layer CBIR approaches depicted in Fig. 5.3(a), Fig. 5.3(b) and Fig. 5.3(c) show the precision, recall and f-score, respectively for COREL dataset and Fig. 5.4(a), Fig. 5.4(b) and Fig. 5.4(c) show the precision, recall and f-score for GHIM dataset. It has been observed from the Fig. 5.3(a) that TSSC feature sequence provide best and consistent results for all the categories of images for COREL dataset.

The retrieval results of CBIR approaches under the three layer model are demonstrated in Fig. 5.5(a), Fig. 5.5(b) and Fig. 5.5(c) for COREL dataset and Fig. 5.6(a), Fig. 5.6(b) and Fig. 5.6(c) shows the performance on GHIM dataset. As observed from Fig. 5.5(a) and Fig. 5.6(a), result are not good for all categories with any of the above mentioned method. Due to this inconsistency in retrieval performance, average retrieval for all the image categories is considered for performance evaluation. It has been observed from the Fig. 5.5(a) that TCS method has high retrieval rate for COREL dataset while CST has for GHIM dataset.

From the above discussion (Table 5.1 and Table 5.2) it can be concluded that the sequence of features texture plus shape at first layer and shape plus color at second layer, $i.e.$, TSSC outperforms all the other sequences in both datasets.

Chapter 5 Implementation Details and Experimental Results 75

5.2.2 Number of Processing Steps in BiCBIR

This section provides analysis of the single layer, bi-layer (proposed) and tri-layer CBIR approaches on the basis of number of processing steps (PS). Total number of steps required for processing are calculated and the best method among each category of CBIR variants is selected. For single layer, bi-layer and tri-layer, *CST1*, *TSSC* and *TCS* approaches are chosen.

Let F_1, F_2 and F_3 be the color, texture and shape feature vectors, respectively. The size of feature vectors F_1, F_2 and F_3 are considered as 81, 60 and 21, respectively.

$$F_1 \approx \frac{4}{3} \times F_2 \tag{5.4}$$

$$F_1 \approx 4 \times F_3 \tag{5.5}$$

$$F_2 \approx 3 \times F_3 \tag{5.6}$$

From the length of feature vectors, Eq. (5.4), Eq. (5.5) and Eq. (5.6) are derived. N is the number of images in the dataset considered for single layer, bi-layer and tri-layer approach.

Single layer approach (CST1): In *CST1*, number of processing steps (PS) required are:

$$PS = N \times [|F_1| + |F_2| + |F_3|] \tag{5.7}$$

By substituting F_1 and F_2 with F_3 from Eq. (5.5) and Eq. (5.6), we get
$PS \approx N \times [4 \times |F_3| + 3 \times |F_3| + |F_3|]$

$$PS \approx 8 \times N \times |F_3| \tag{5.8}$$

Bi-layer approach (TSSC): Total number of steps required are:

$$PS = N \times [|F_2| + |F_3|] + \frac{N}{5} \times [|F_1| + |F_3|] \tag{5.9}$$

Chapter 5 Implementation Details and Experimental Results

By substituting $|F_1|$ and $|F_2|$ with $|F_3|$ from Eq. (5.5) and Eq. (5.6), we get Eq. (5.12)

$$PS \approx N \times [3 \times |F_3| + |F_3|] + \frac{N}{5} \times [4 \times |F_3| + |F_3|] \qquad (5.10)$$

$$PS \approx N \times [4 \times |F_3|] + \frac{N}{5} \times [5 \times |F_3|] \qquad (5.11)$$

$$PS \approx 5 \times N \times |F_3| \qquad (5.12)$$

From Eq. 5.8 and Eq. 5.12 it is observed that $TSSC$ takes only 0.625 times of PS as compared to $CTS1$.

Tri-layer approach (TSC): Processing steps required in TSC are:

$$PS = N \times |F_2| + \frac{N}{10} \times |F_1| + \frac{N}{20} \times |F_3| \qquad (5.13)$$

By substituting $|F_1|$ and $|F_2|$ with $|F_3|$ from Eq. (5.5) and Eq. (5.6), we get Eq. (5.14)

$$PS \approx N \times 3 \times |F_3| + \frac{N}{10} \times 4 \times |F_3| + \frac{N}{20} \times |F_3| \qquad (5.14)$$

$$PS \approx \frac{69 \times N \times |F_3|}{20} \qquad (5.15)$$

$$PS \approx 3.45 \times N \times |F_3| \qquad (5.16)$$

From Eq. 5.8, Eq. 5.12 and Eq. 5.16 it is observed that the TSC takes less than half of PS as compared to $CTS1$ and slightly lesser than the proposed approach ($TSSC$). $TSSC$ takes slightly more number of processing steps as compared to TCS but this extra computational cost provides 10% (Table 5.1) higher average precision for Wang dataset and 17% (Table 5.2) for GHIM dataset. On the basis of precision rate and processing steps, $TSSC$ is selected as proposed BiCBIR method. Further it is compared with other state-of-the-art CBIR methods.

Table 5.1: Performance of CBIR variants on COREL dataset in terms of precision, recall and f-score

Class	Evaluation	C	T	S	CTS1	TCCS	CTTS	CSST	SCCT	STTC	TSSC	CTS	CST	TCS	TSC	STC	SCT
Africa	Precision	0.500	0.550	0.700	0.850	0.900	0.700	0.950	0.950	0.650	0.950	0.850	0.850	0.850	0.900	0.900	0.800
	Recall	0.100	0.110	0.140	0.170	0.180	0.140	0.190	0.190	0.130	0.190	0.170	0.170	0.170	0.180	0.180	0.160
	F-score	0.167	0.183	0.233	0.283	0.300	0.233	0.317	0.317	0.217	0.317	0.283	0.283	0.283	0.300	0.300	0.267
Beach	Precision	0.450	0.550	0.550	0.650	0.650	0.500	0.700	0.650	0.400	0.750	0.500	0.600	0.550	0.550	0.650	0.650
	Recall	0.090	0.110	0.110	0.130	0.130	0.100	0.140	0.130	0.080	0.150	0.100	0.120	0.110	0.110	0.130	0.130
	F-score	0.150	0.183	0.183	0.217	0.217	0.167	0.233	0.217	0.133	0.250	0.167	0.200	0.183	0.183	0.217	0.217
Building	Precision	0.400	0.700	0.650	0.800	0.700	0.650	0.700	0.700	0.700	0.850	0.500	0.600	0.700	0.600	0.750	0.800
	Recall	0.080	0.140	0.130	0.160	0.140	0.130	0.140	0.140	0.140	0.170	0.100	0.120	0.140	0.120	0.150	0.160
	F-score	0.133	0.233	0.217	0.267	0.233	0.217	0.233	0.233	0.233	0.283	0.167	0.200	0.233	0.200	0.250	0.267
Bus	Precision	0.500	0.650	0.500	1.000	1.000	0.750	1.000	1.000	0.550	1.000	0.800	0.950	0.850	1.000	1.000	0.850
	Recall	0.100	0.130	0.100	0.200	0.200	0.150	0.200	0.200	0.110	0.200	0.160	0.190	0.170	0.200	0.200	0.170
	F-score	0.167	0.217	0.167	0.333	0.333	0.250	0.333	0.333	0.183	0.333	0.267	0.317	0.283	0.333	0.333	0.283
Dinosaur	Precision	0.550	0.600	0.950	0.950	0.950	0.950	1.000	1.000	0.900	1.000	1.000	1.000	1.000	0.950	0.950	0.900
	Recall	0.110	0.120	0.190	0.190	0.190	0.190	0.200	0.200	0.180	0.200	0.200	0.200	0.200	0.190	0.190	0.180
	F-score	0.183	0.200	0.317	0.317	0.317	0.317	0.333	0.333	0.300	0.333	0.333	0.333	0.333	0.317	0.317	0.300
Elephant	Precision	0.450	0.600	0.600	0.900	0.650	0.900	0.850	0.700	0.800	0.900	0.750	0.750	0.800	0.750	0.700	0.750
	Recall	0.090	0.120	0.120	0.180	0.130	0.180	0.170	0.140	0.160	0.180	0.150	0.150	0.160	0.150	0.140	0.150
	F-score	0.150	0.200	0.200	0.300	0.217	0.300	0.283	0.233	0.267	0.300	0.250	0.250	0.267	0.250	0.233	0.250
Flower	Precision	0.550	0.800	0.850	1.000	0.950	0.900	1.000	0.900	0.650	1.000	1.000	0.950	1.000	0.850	0.850	0.850
	Recall	0.110	0.160	0.170	0.200	0.190	0.180	0.200	0.180	0.130	0.200	0.200	0.190	0.200	0.170	0.170	0.170
	F-score	0.183	0.267	0.283	0.333	0.317	0.300	0.333	0.300	0.217	0.333	0.333	0.317	0.333	0.283	0.283	0.283
Horse	Precision	0.750	0.650	0.650	0.900	0.950	0.700	1.000	0.900	0.850	1.000	1.000	0.950	0.900	0.950	0.950	0.950
	Recall	0.150	0.130	0.130	0.180	0.190	0.140	0.200	0.180	0.170	0.200	0.200	0.190	0.180	0.190	0.190	0.190
	F-score	0.250	0.217	0.217	0.300	0.317	0.233	0.333	0.300	0.283	0.333	0.333	0.317	0.300	0.317	0.317	0.317
Mountain	Precision	0.600	0.750	0.700	0.500	0.750	0.800	0.500	0.750	0.750	0.800	0.550	0.600	0.750	0.650	0.600	0.700

Continued on next page

Table 5.1 – (Continued)

Class	Evaluation	C	T	S	CTS1	TCCS	CTTS	CSST	SCCT	STTC	TSSC	CTS	CST	TCS	TSC	STC	SCT
Food	Recall	0.120	0.150	0.140	0.100	0.150	0.160	0.100	0.150	0.150	0.160	0.110	0.120	0.150	0.130	0.120	0.140
	F-score	0.200	0.250	0.233	0.167	0.250	0.267	0.167	0.250	0.250	0.267	0.183	0.200	0.250	0.217	0.200	0.233
	Precision	0.800	0.700	0.750	0.800	0.950	0.750	0.850	0.900	0.650	0.950	0.800	0.850	0.850	1.000	0.850	0.850
	Recall	0.160	0.140	0.150	0.160	0.190	0.150	0.170	0.180	0.130	0.190	0.160	0.170	0.170	0.200	0.170	0.170
	F-score	0.267	0.233	0.250	0.267	0.317	0.250	0.283	0.300	0.217	0.317	0.267	0.283	0.283	0.333	0.283	0.283
Average	Precision	0.555	0.655	0.690	0.835	0.845	0.760	0.855	0.825	0.690	0.920	0.775	0.810	0.825	0.820	0.820	0.810
	Recall	0.111	0.131	0.138	0.167	0.169	0.152	0.171	0.165	0.138	0.184	0.155	0.162	0.165	0.164	0.164	0.162
	F-score	0.185	0.218	0.230	0.278	0.282	0.253	0.285	0.275	0.230	0.307	0.258	0.270	0.275	0.273	0.273	0.270

Table 5.2: Performance of CBIR variants on GHIM dataset in terms of precision, recall and f-score

Class	Evaluation	C	T	S	CTS1	TCCS	CTTS	CSST	SCCT	STTC	TSSC	CTS	CST	TCS	TSC	STC	SCT
Fireworks	Precision	0.500	0.600	0.750	0.900	0.850	0.800	0.950	0.850	0.650	0.950	1.000	0.950	0.950	0.850	0.850	0.900
	Recall	0.100	0.120	0.150	0.180	0.170	0.160	0.190	0.170	0.130	0.190	0.200	0.190	0.190	0.170	0.170	0.180
	F-score	0.167	0.200	0.250	0.300	0.283	0.267	0.317	0.283	0.217	0.317	0.333	0.317	0.317	0.283	0.283	0.300
Building	Precision	0.550	0.750	0.300	0.850	0.750	0.850	0.850	0.900	0.650	0.900	0.750	0.800	0.850	0.750	0.750	0.850
	Recall	0.110	0.150	0.060	0.170	0.150	0.170	0.170	0.180	0.130	0.180	0.150	0.160	0.170	0.150	0.150	0.170
	F-score	0.183	0.250	0.100	0.283	0.250	0.283	0.283	0.300	0.217	0.300	0.250	0.267	0.283	0.250	0.250	0.283
Wall	Precision	0.350	0.300	0.400	0.350	0.550	0.700	0.700	0.600	0.500	0.750	0.500	0.550	0.600	0.550	0.750	0.600
	Recall	0.070	0.060	0.080	0.070	0.110	0.140	0.140	0.120	0.100	0.150	0.100	0.110	0.120	0.110	0.150	0.120
	F-score	0.117	0.100	0.133	0.117	0.183	0.233	0.233	0.200	0.167	0.250	0.167	0.183	0.200	0.183	0.250	0.200
Car	Precision	0.600	0.650	0.400	0.850	0.650	0.800	0.800	0.700	0.650	0.900	0.700	0.750	0.850	0.800	0.700	0.850
	Recall	0.120	0.130	0.080	0.170	0.130	0.160	0.160	0.140	0.130	0.180	0.140	0.150	0.170	0.160	0.140	0.170
	F-score	0.200	0.217	0.133	0.283	0.217	0.267	0.267	0.233	0.217	0.300	0.233	0.250	0.283	0.267	0.233	0.283
Bees	Precision	0.500	0.750	0.450	0.900	0.750	0.750	0.750	0.650	0.800	0.950	0.650	0.700	0.550	0.650	0.600	0.600
	Recall	0.100	0.150	0.090	0.180	0.150	0.150	0.150	0.130	0.160	0.190	0.130	0.140	0.110	0.130	0.120	0.120
	F-score	0.167	0.250	0.150	0.300	0.250	0.250	0.250	0.217	0.267	0.317	0.217	0.233	0.183	0.217	0.200	0.200
Mountains	Precision	0.950	0.400	0.650	0.900	1.000	0.450	0.800	0.950	0.350	1.000	0.550	0.650	0.550	0.550	0.500	0.450
	Recall	0.190	0.080	0.130	0.180	0.200	0.090	0.160	0.190	0.070	0.200	0.110	0.130	0.110	0.110	0.100	0.090
	F-score	0.317	0.133	0.217	0.300	0.333	0.150	0.267	0.317	0.117	0.333	0.183	0.217	0.183	0.183	0.167	0.150
Flowers	Precision	0.600	0.850	0.450	0.800	1.000	0.950	1.000	1.000	0.950	1.000	0.950	1.000	0.950	0.900	0.900	1.000
	Recall	0.120	0.170	0.090	0.160	0.200	0.190	0.200	0.200	0.190	0.200	0.190	0.200	0.190	0.180	0.180	0.200
	F-score	0.200	0.283	0.150	0.267	0.333	0.317	0.333	0.333	0.317	0.333	0.317	0.333	0.317	0.300	0.300	0.333
Trees	Precision	0.550	0.450	0.850	0.800	0.850	0.600	0.750	0.750	0.400	0.900	0.550	0.700	0.650	0.650	0.600	0.550
	Recall	0.110	0.090	0.170	0.160	0.170	0.120	0.150	0.150	0.080	0.180	0.110	0.140	0.130	0.130	0.120	0.110
	F-score	0.183	0.150	0.283	0.267	0.283	0.200	0.250	0.250	0.133	0.300	0.183	0.233	0.217	0.217	0.200	0.183
Fields	Precision	0.700	0.550	0.650	0.850	0.950	0.750	0.850	0.900	0.500	0.900	0.700	0.600	0.750	0.700	0.500	0.600

Continued on next page

Table 5.2 – (Continued)

Class	Evaluation	C	T	S	CTS1	TCCS	CTTS	CSST	SCCT	STTC	TSSC	CTS	CST	TCS	TSC	STC	SCT
Beaches	Recall	0.140	0.110	0.130	0.170	0.190	0.150	0.170	0.180	0.100	0.180	0.140	0.120	0.150	0.140	0.100	0.120
	F-score	0.233	0.183	0.217	0.283	0.317	0.250	0.283	0.300	0.167	0.300	0.233	0.200	0.250	0.233	0.167	0.200
	Precision	0.600	0.750	0.650	0.650	0.600	0.600	0.600	0.700	0.400	0.750	0.650	0.700	0.650	0.700	0.500	0.500
	Recall	0.120	0.150	0.130	0.130	0.120	0.120	0.120	0.140	0.080	0.150	0.130	0.140	0.130	0.140	0.100	0.100
	F-score	0.200	0.250	0.217	0.217	0.200	0.200	0.200	0.233	0.133	0.250	0.217	0.233	0.217	0.233	0.167	0.167
Average	Precision	0.590	0.605	0.555	0.785	0.795	0.725	0.805	0.800	0.585	0.900	0.700	0.740	0.735	0.710	0.665	0.690
	Recall	0.118	0.121	0.111	0.157	0.159	0.145	0.161	0.160	0.117	0.180	0.140	0.148	0.147	0.142	0.133	0.138
	F-score	0.197	0.202	0.185	0.262	0.265	0.242	0.268	0.267	0.195	0.300	0.233	0.247	0.245	0.237	0.222	0.230

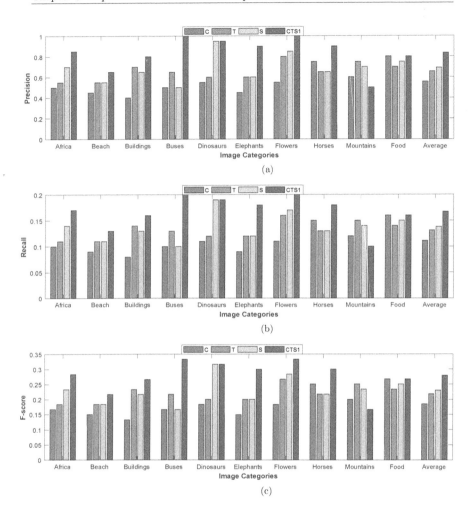

Figure 5.1: Precision: 5.1(a), recall: 5.1(b) and f-score 5.1(c) of single layer CBIR variants for Wang dataset

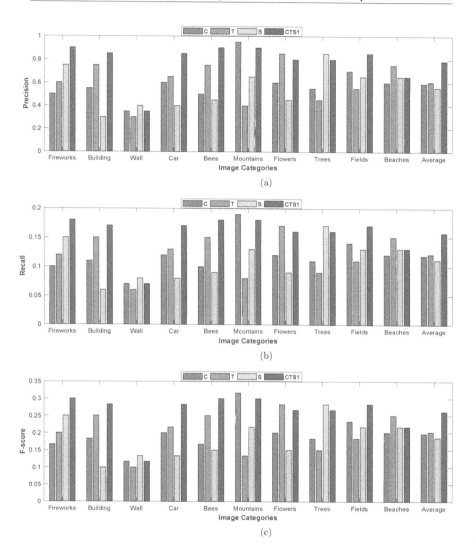

Figure 5.2: Precision: 5.2(a), recall: 5.2(b) and f-score 5.2(c) of single layer CBIR variants for GHIM dataset

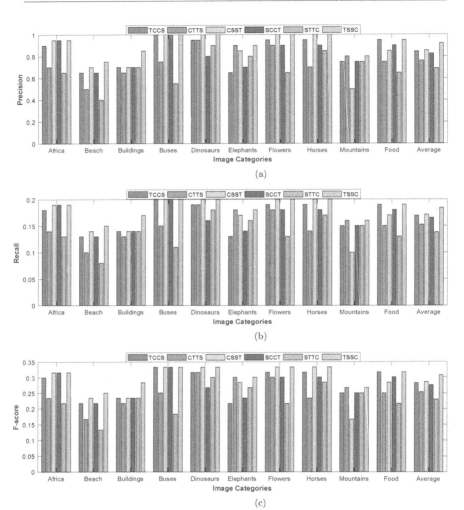

Figure 5.3: Precision: 5.3(a), recall: 5.3(b) and f-score 5.3(c) of bi-layer CBIR variants for GHIM dataset

5.2.3 Comparison of BiCBIR with Other Approaches

The proposed BiCBIR approach has been compared with of the existing CBIR systems (Table 5.3). Elalami *et al.* [161] proposed the integration of the color coherence vector

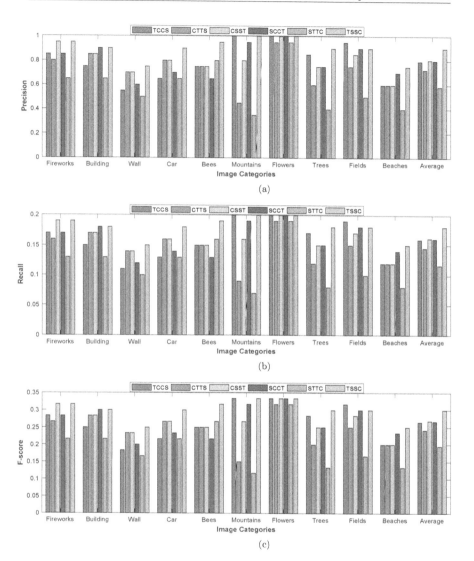

Figure 5.4: Precision: 5.4(a), recall: 5.4(b) and f-score 5.4(c) of bi-layer CBIR variants for GHIM dataset

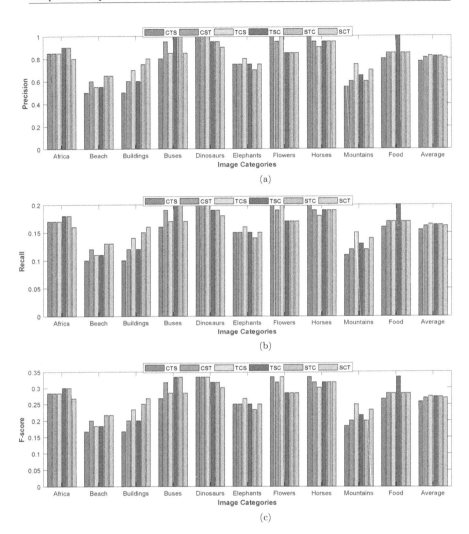

Figure 5.5: Precision: 5.5(a), recall: 5.5(b) and f-score 5.5(c) of tri-layer CBIR variants for Wang dataset

and wavelet features to enhance the retrieval performance. Zeng et al. [162] compute the similarity between two spatiograms through a similarity measure function based

Chapter 5 Implementation Details and Experimental Results

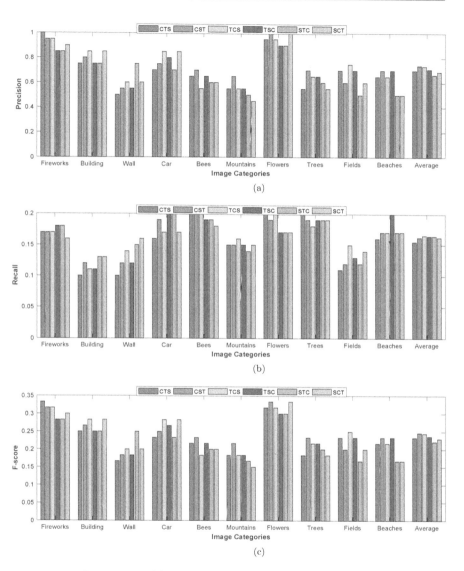

Figure 5.6: Precision: 5.6(a), recall: 5.6(b) and f-score 5.6(c) of tri-layer CBIR variants for GHIM dataset

Chapter 5 Implementation Details and Experimental Results   **87**

on Jensen–Shannon Divergence. Guo and Prasetyo [163] proposed two image features, color co-occurrence and bit pattern features. To achieve fast search, images were indexed directly from the ordered-dither block truncation coding without performing the decoding process. CBIR system proposed by Lande *et al.* [164] uses color, texture, and shape features of an image. The extracted features were combined to improve the efficacy for matching and retrieval purpose. Pradhan *et al.* [94] proposed a hierarchical CBIR system which consists of three layers and uses three image features, *i.e.*, color, texture and shape. This hierarchical CBIR model reduced the search space at each layer by removing the non-relevant images to achieve high retrieval speed.

It is evident from Fig 5.7(a) that in the nine categories of images considered, precision of the proposed approach (BiCBIR) is better or equal in COREL dataset. Recall and f-score are shown in Fig 5.7(b) and Fig 5.7(c), respectively. Results are provided in Table 5.3 to quantify the efficiency of the proposed CBIR approach, which shows that average retrieval in BiCBIR is better in all the image categories than the other CBIR systems. In Table 5.3, precision, recall and f-score of the proposed approach has been depicted along with other state-of-the-art methods.

Space complexity of BiCBIR: BiCBIR uses two layers for image retrieval and three types of image feature: at first layer it uses two features, say F_1 and F_2, and at second layer two features F_2 and F_3 are used.

Case I: Memory required to store database consisting of features extracted from N images (for similarity computation) is $N \times (|F_1| + |F_2| + |F_3|)$

Case II: Memory required in layered approach is $N \times max((|F_1| + |F_2|), (|F_1| + |F_3|), (|F_2| + |F_3|))$ (Considering various combinations of features). Thus memory required in Case II is always less than that required in Case I.

Table 5.3: Comparison of proposed BiCBIR approach with five other CBIR systems on COREL dataset in terms of precision, recall and f-score.

Class	Evaluation	Elalami [161]	Zeng et al. [162]	Guo et al. [163]	Lande et al. [164]	Pradhan et al. [94]	BiCBIR (Proposed)
Africa	Precision	0.562	0.725	0.847	0.750	0.950	0.950
	Recall	0.112	0.145	0.169	0.150	0.190	0.190
	F-score	0.187	0.242	0.282	0.250	0.317	0.317
Beach	Precision	0.536	0.652	0.466	0.550	0.600	0.750
	Recall	0.107	0.130	0.093	0.110	0.120	0.150
	F-score	0.179	0.217	0.155	0.183	0.200	0.250
Building	Precision	0.610	0.706	0.682	0.750	0.550	0.850
	Recall	0.122	0.141	0.136	0.150	0.110	0.170
	F-score	0.203	0.235	0.227	0.250	0.183	0.283
Bus	Precision	0.893	0.892	0.885	0.550	1.000	1.000
	Recall	0.179	0.178	0.177	0.110	0.200	0.200
	F-score	0.298	0.297	0.295	0.183	0.333	0.333
Dinosaur	Precision	0.984	1.000	0.992	1.000	1.000	1.000
	Recall	0.197	0.200	0.198	0.200	0.200	0.200
	F-score	0.328	0.333	0.331	0.333	0.333	0.333
Elephant	Precision	0.578	0.705	0.733	0.750	0.900	0.900
	Recall	0.116	0.141	0.147	0.150	0.180	0.180
	F-score	0.193	0.235	0.244	0.250	0.300	0.300
Flower	Precision	0.899	0.948	0.964	0.850	1.000	1.000
	Recall	0.180	0.190	0.193	0.170	0.200	0.200
	F-score	0.300	0.316	0.321	0.283	0.333	0.333
Horse	Precision	0.780	0.918	0.939	0.900	1.000	1.000
	Recall	0.156	0.184	0.188	0.180	0.200	0.200
	F-score	0.260	0.306	0.313	0.300	0.333	0.333
Mountain	Precision	0.512	0.723	0.474	0.500	0.750	0.800
	Recall	0.102	0.145	0.095	0.100	0.150	0.160
	F-score	0.171	0.241	0.158	0.167	0.250	0.267
Food	Precision	0.693	0.788	0.806	0.750	1.000	0.950
	Recall	0.139	0.158	0.161	0.150	0.200	0.190
	F-score	0.231	0.263	0.269	0.250	0.333	0.317
Average	Precision	0.705	0.806	0.779	0.735	0.875	0.920
	Recall	0.141	0.161	0.156	0.147	0.175	0.184
	F-score	0.235	0.269	0.260	0.245	0.292	0.307

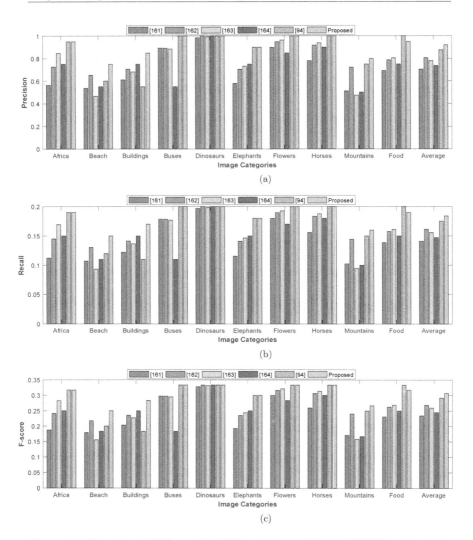

Figure 5.7: Precision: 5.7(a), recall: 5.7(b) and f-score 5.7(c) of BiCBIR and existing CBIR approaches for Wang dataset

5.3 Experimental Results of FiCBIR

The retrieval performance of the proposed layer-wise feature incremental approach has been tested on four datasets (Section 5.1.2) which contain variety of images. Experiment has been performed with thirteen possible combinations which are based on feature(s) used in different layers. Description of feature(s) is provided in Table 4.5.

Table 5.4: Performance of the FiCBIR approach with other variants on Wang dataset in terms of precision, recall and f-score.

Class	Evaluation	M1	M2	M3	M4	M5	M6	M7	M8	M9	M10	M11	M12	M13
Africa	Precision	0.900	0.800	0.800	0.850	0.900	0.750	0.900	**0.950**	0.500	0.900	0.900	0.600	0.850
	Recall	0.180	0.160	0.160	0.170	0.180	0.150	0.180	**0.190**	0.100	0.180	0.180	0.120	0.170
	F-score	0.300	0.267	0.267	0.283	0.300	0.250	0.300	**0.317**	0.167	0.300	0.300	0.200	0.283
Beach	Precision	0.800	0.550	0.500	0.550	0.700	0.500	0.650	**0.800**	0.400	0.700	0.600	0.750	0.650
	Recall	0.160	0.110	0.100	0.110	0.140	0.100	0.130	**0.160**	0.080	0.140	0.120	0.150	0.130
	F-score	0.267	0.183	0.167	0.183	0.233	0.167	0.217	**0.267**	0.133	0.233	0.200	0.250	0.217
Building	Precision	0.800	0.600	0.650	0.500	0.600	0.500	0.500	**0.950**	0.300	0.800	0.850	0.350	0.500
	Recall	0.160	0.120	0.130	0.100	0.120	0.100	0.100	**0.190**	0.060	0.160	0.170	0.070	0.100
	F-score	0.267	0.200	0.217	0.167	0.200	0.167	0.167	**0.317**	0.100	0.267	0.283	0.117	0.167
Bus	Precision	1.000	0.850	0.950	0.800	1.000	0.850	1.000	**1.000**	0.900	1.000	0.700	0.800	0.850
	Recall	0.200	0.170	0.190	0.160	0.200	0.170	0.200	**0.200**	0.180	0.200	0.140	0.160	0.170
	F-score	0.333	0.283	0.317	0.267	0.333	0.283	0.333	**0.333**	0.300	0.333	0.233	0.267	0.283
Dinosaur	Precision	1.000	1.000	0.950	1.000	0.850	0.850	0.850	**1.000**	1.000	1.000	1.000	0.850	1.000
	Recall	0.200	0.200	0.190	0.200	0.170	0.170	0.170	**0.200**	0.200	0.200	0.200	0.170	0.200
	F-score	0.333	0.333	0.317	0.333	0.283	0.283	0.283	**0.333**	0.333	0.333	0.333	0.283	0.333
Elephant	Precision	0.900	0.850	0.800	0.800	0.800	0.850	0.800	**0.900**	0.650	0.900	0.900	0.400	0.900
	Recall	0.180	0.170	0.160	0.160	0.160	0.170	0.160	**0.180**	0.130	0.180	0.180	0.080	0.180
	F-score	0.300	0.283	0.267	0.267	0.267	0.283	0.267	**0.300**	0.217	0.300	0.300	0.133	0.300
Flower	Precision	1.000	1.000	0.950	1.000	0.850	0.850	0.850	**1.000**	1.000	1.000	1.000	0.650	0.900
	Recall	0.200	0.200	0.190	0.200	0.170	0.170	0.170	**0.200**	0.200	0.200	0.200	0.130	0.180
	F-score	0.333	0.333	0.317	0.333	0.283	0.283	0.283	**0.333**	0.333	0.333	0.333	0.217	0.300
Horse	Precision	1.000	0.900	0.950	0.900	0.950	0.950	0.950	**1.000**	0.800	1.000	0.900	0.950	0.900
	Recall	0.200	0.180	0.190	0.180	0.190	0.190	0.190	**0.200**	0.160	0.200	0.180	0.190	0.180
	F-score	0.333	0.300	0.317	0.300	0.317	0.317	0.317	**0.333**	0.267	0.333	0.300	0.317	0.300

(Continued on next page)

Table 5.4 – (Continued)

Class	Evaluation	M1	M2	M3	M4	M5	M6	M7	M8	M9	M10	M11	M12	M13
Mountain	Precision	0.750	0.550	0.550	0.550	0.600	0.500	0.500	**0.750**	0.600	0.750	0.450	0.550	0.500
	Recall	0.150	0.110	0.110	0.110	0.120	0.100	0.100	**0.150**	0.120	0.150	0.090	0.110	0.100
	F-score	0.250	0.183	0.183	0.183	0.200	0.167	0.167	**0.250**	0.200	0.250	0.150	0.183	0.167
Food	Precision	0.950	0.650	0.700	0.650	0.650	0.700	0.650	**1.000**	0.250	0.950	0.950	0.400	0.750
	Recall	0.190	0.130	0.140	0.130	0.130	0.140	0.130	**0.200**	0.050	0.190	0.190	0.080	0.150
	F-score	0.317	0.217	0.233	0.217	0.217	0.233	0.217	**0.333**	0.083	0.317	0.317	0.133	0.250
Average	Precision	0.910	0.775	0.780	0.760	0.790	0.730	0.765	**0.935**	0.640	0.900	0.825	0.630	0.780
	Recall	0.182	0.155	0.156	0.152	0.158	0.146	0.153	**0.187**	0.128	0.180	0.165	0.126	0.156
	F-score	0.303	0.258	0.260	0.253	0.263	0.243	0.255	**0.312**	0.213	0.300	0.275	0.210	0.260

Table 5.5: Performance of FiCBIR approach with other variants on GHIM-10k dataset in terms of precision, recall and f-score.

Class	Evaluation	M1	M2	M3	M4	M5	M6	M7	M8	M9	M10	M11	M12	M13
Fireworks	Precision	1.000	0.950	1.000	0.950	0.950	0.950	0.900	**1.000**	0.800	0.950	0.950	0.750	0.950
	Recall	0.040	0.038	0.040	0.038	0.038	0.038	0.036	**0.040**	0.032	0.038	0.038	0.030	0.038
	F-score	0.077	0.073	0.077	0.073	0.073	0.073	0.069	**0.077**	0.062	0.073	0.073	0.058	0.073
Building	Precision	0.800	0.600	0.650	0.500	0.550	0.700	0.500	**0.900**	0.300	0.800	0.900	0.250	0.750
	Recall	0.032	0.024	0.026	0.020	0.022	0.028	0.020	**0.036**	0.012	0.032	0.036	0.010	0.030
	F-score	0.062	0.046	0.050	0.038	0.042	0.054	0.038	**0.069**	0.023	0.062	0.069	0.019	0.058
Wall	Precision	0.550	0.500	0.400	0.450	0.500	0.450	0.400	**0.650**	0.350	0.350	0.300	0.350	0.400
	Recall	0.022	0.020	0.016	0.018	0.020	0.018	0.016	**0.026**	0.014	0.014	0.012	0.014	0.016
	F-score	0.042	0.038	0.031	0.035	0.038	0.035	0.031	**0.050**	0.027	0.027	0.023	0.027	0.031
Car	Precision	0.750	0.500	0.650	0.600	0.650	0.500	0.400	**0.750**	0.550	0.600	0.550	0.650	0.500
	Recall	0.030	0.020	0.026	0.024	0.026	0.020	0.016	**0.030**	0.022	0.024	0.022	0.026	0.020
	F-score	0.058	0.038	0.050	0.046	0.050	0.038	0.031	**0.058**	0.042	0.046	0.042	0.050	0.038
Bees	Precision	**0.950**	0.650	0.750	0.700	0.650	0.600	0.700	0.800	0.700	0.800	0.700	0.750	0.650
	Recall	**0.038**	0.026	0.030	0.028	0.026	0.024	0.028	0.032	0.028	0.032	0.028	0.030	0.026
	F-score	**0.073**	0.050	0.058	0.054	0.050	0.046	0.054	0.062	0.054	0.062	0.054	0.058	0.050
Mountains	Precision	0.900	0.400	0.600	0.400	0.600	0.750	0.700	**0.950**	0.950	0.850	0.700	0.500	0.650
	Recall	0.036	0.016	0.024	0.016	0.024	0.030	0.028	**0.038**	0.038	0.034	0.028	0.020	0.026
	F-score	0.069	0.031	0.046	0.031	0.046	0.058	0.054	**0.073**	0.073	0.065	0.054	0.038	0.050
Flowers	Precision	0.850	0.900	0.900	0.800	0.950	0.800	0.800	**1.000**	0.550	1.000	0.950	0.550	1.000
	Recall	0.034	0.036	0.036	0.032	0.038	0.032	0.032	**0.040**	0.022	0.040	0.038	0.022	0.040
	F-score	0.065	0.069	0.069	0.062	0.073	0.062	0.062	**0.077**	0.042	0.077	0.073	0.042	0.077
Trees	Precision	0.900	0.550	0.600	0.600	0.650	0.600	0.500	**0.900**	0.250	0.850	0.850	0.200	0.600
	Recall	0.036	0.022	0.024	0.024	0.026	0.024	0.020	**0.036**	0.010	0.034	0.034	0.008	0.024
	F-score	0.069	0.042	0.046	0.046	0.050	0.046	0.038	**0.069**	0.019	0.065	0.065	0.015	0.046

Continued on next page

Table 5.5 – (Continued)

Class	Evaluation	M1	M2	M3	M4	M5	M6	M7	M8	M9	M10	M11	M12	M13
Fields	Precision	0.950	0.650	0.750	0.650	0.600	0.700	0.700	**0.950**	0.850	0.850	0.550	0.550	0.700
	Recall	0.038	0.026	0.030	0.026	0.024	0.028	0.028	**0.038**	0.034	0.034	0.022	0.022	0.028
	F-score	0.073	0.050	0.058	0.050	0.046	0.054	0.054	**0.073**	0.065	0.065	0.042	0.042	0.054
Beaches	Precision	0.650	0.500	0.650	0.600	0.650	0.500	0.400	**0.750**	0.550	0.600	0.550	0.650	0.500
	Recall	0.026	0.020	0.026	0.024	0.026	0.020	0.016	**0.030**	0.022	0.024	0.022	0.026	0.020
	F-score	0.050	0.038	0.050	0.046	0.050	0.038	0.031	**0.058**	0.042	0.046	0.042	0.050	0.038
Planes	Precision	0.800	0.650	0.750	0.700	0.650	0.600	0.700	**0.800**	0.700	0.800	0.700	0.750	0.650
	Recall	0.032	0.026	0.030	0.028	0.026	0.024	0.028	**0.032**	0.028	0.032	0.028	0.030	0.026
	F-score	0.062	0.050	0.058	0.054	0.050	0.046	0.054	**0.062**	0.054	0.062	0.054	0.058	0.050
Butter Fly	Precision	0.650	0.550	0.700	0.450	0.750	0.500	0.400	**0.700**	0.450	0.700	0.700	0.500	0.600
	Recall	0.026	0.022	0.028	0.018	0.030	0.020	0.016	**0.028**	0.018	0.028	0.028	0.020	0.024
	F-score	0.050	0.042	0.054	0.035	0.058	0.038	0.031	**0.054**	0.035	0.054	0.054	0.038	0.046
Chiness Structure	Precision	0.600	0.550	0.550	0.650	0.550	0.300	0.500	**0.750**	0.500	0.550	0.750	0.400	0.650
	Recall	0.024	0.022	0.022	0.026	0.022	0.012	0.020	**0.030**	0.020	0.022	0.030	0.016	0.026
	F-score	0.046	0.042	0.042	0.050	0.042	0.023	0.038	**0.058**	0.038	0.042	0.058	0.031	0.050
Sunset	Precision	0.950	0.450	0.900	0.500	0.850	0.500	0.600	**0.950**	0.900	0.800	0.650	0.500	0.500
	Recall	0.038	0.018	0.036	0.020	0.034	0.020	0.024	**0.038**	0.036	0.032	0.026	0.020	0.020
	F-score	0.073	0.035	0.069	0.038	0.065	0.038	0.046	**0.073**	0.069	0.062	0.050	0.038	0.038
Bikes	Precision	0.900	0.500	0.700	0.550	0.900	0.450	0.550	**1.000**	0.250	0.900	0.850	0.550	0.600
	Recall	0.036	0.020	0.028	0.022	0.036	0.018	0.022	**0.040**	0.010	0.036	0.034	0.022	0.024
	F-score	0.069	0.038	0.054	0.042	0.069	0.035	0.042	**0.077**	0.019	0.069	0.065	0.042	0.046
Boats	Precision	0.900	0.550	0.750	0.600	0.850	0.500	0.700	**0.950**	0.400	0.950	0.950	0.600	0.600
	Recall	0.036	0.022	0.030	0.024	0.034	0.020	0.028	**0.038**	0.016	0.038	0.038	0.024	0.024
	F-score	0.069	0.042	0.058	0.046	0.065	0.038	0.054	**0.073**	0.031	0.073	0.073	0.046	0.046
Ships	Precision	**0.750**	0.550	0.650	0.550	0.600	0.600	0.500	0.600	0.450	0.400	0.250	0.700	0.400
	Recall	**0.030**	0.022	0.026	0.022	0.024	0.024	0.020	0.024	0.018	0.016	0.010	0.028	0.016

Continued on next page

Table 5.5 – (Continued)

Class	Evaluation	M1	M2	M3	M4	M5	M6	M7	M8	M9	M10	M11	M12	M13
	F-score	**0.058**	0.042	0.050	0.042	0.046	0.046	0.038	0.046	0.035	0.031	0.019	0.054	0.031
Chicken	Precision	0.700	0.700	0.650	0.400	0.750	0.550	0.750	**0.900**	0.450	0.700	0.650	0.650	0.800
	Recall	0.028	0.028	0.026	0.016	0.030	0.022	0.030	**0.036**	0.018	0.028	0.026	0.026	0.032
	F-score	0.054	0.054	0.050	0.031	0.058	0.042	0.058	**0.069**	0.035	0.054	0.050	0.050	0.062
Insects	Precision	0.650	0.800	0.600	0.400	0.500	0.400	0.600	**0.850**	0.750	0.500	0.450	0.700	0.550
	Recall	0.026	0.032	0.024	0.016	0.020	0.016	0.024	**0.034**	0.030	0.020	0.018	0.028	0.022
	F-score	0.050	0.062	0.046	0.031	0.038	0.031	0.046	**0.065**	0.058	0.038	0.035	0.054	0.042
Hourse	Precision	**0.900**	0.550	0.850	0.550	0.450	0.450	0.650	0.850	0.850	0.500	0.300	0.600	0.700
	Recall	**0.036**	0.022	0.034	0.022	0.018	0.018	0.026	0.034	0.034	0.020	0.012	0.024	0.028
	F-score	**0.069**	0.042	0.065	0.042	0.035	0.035	0.050	0.065	0.065	0.038	0.023	0.046	0.054
Average	Precision	0.805	0.615	0.708	0.568	0.673	0.573	0.603	**0.865**	0.560	0.738	0.673	0.540	0.653
	Recall	0.032	0.025	0.028	0.023	0.027	0.023	0.024	**0.035**	0.022	0.030	0.027	0.022	0.026
	F-score	0.062	0.047	0.054	0.044	0.052	0.044	0.046	**0.067**	0.043	0.057	0.052	0.042	0.050

Table 5.6: Performance of FiCBIR approach with other variants on COREL dataset in terms of precision, recall and f-score.

Class	Evaluation	M1	M2	M3	M4	M5	M6	M7	M8	M9	M10	M11	M12	M13
God	Precision	1.000	0.900	0.900	0.900	0.950	1.000	0.950	**1.000**	0.900	1.000	1.000	0.750	0.900
	Recall	0.200	0.180	0.180	0.180	0.190	0.200	0.190	**0.200**	0.180	0.200	0.200	0.150	0.180
	F-score	0.333	0.300	0.300	0.300	0.317	0.333	0.317	**0.333**	0.300	0.333	0.333	0.250	0.300
Bear	Precision	0.850	0.650	0.650	0.650	0.650	0.650	0.650	0.850	0.450	0.750	0.700	0.300	**0.900**
	Recall	0.170	0.130	0.130	0.130	0.130	0.130	0.130	0.170	0.090	0.150	0.140	0.060	**0.180**
	F-score	0.283	0.217	0.217	0.217	0.217	0.217	0.217	0.283	0.150	0.250	0.233	0.100	**0.300**
Jackal	Precision	0.700	0.500	0.600	0.400	0.550	0.500	0.500	0.700	0.700	**0.750**	0.350	0.550	0.350
	Recall	0.140	0.100	0.120	0.080	0.110	0.100	0.100	0.140	0.140	**0.150**	0.070	0.110	0.070
	F-score	0.233	0.167	0.200	0.133	0.183	0.167	0.167	0.233	0.233	**0.250**	0.117	0.183	0.117
Lion	Precision	0.650	0.550	0.500	0.350	0.650	0.600	0.600	**0.900**	0.150	0.900	0.900	0.250	0.400
	Recall	0.130	0.110	0.100	0.070	0.130	0.120	0.120	**0.180**	0.030	0.180	0.180	0.050	0.080
	F-score	0.217	0.183	0.167	0.117	0.217	0.200	0.200	**0.300**	0.050	0.300	0.300	0.083	0.133
Elephant	Precision	**0.900**	0.450	0.450	0.150	0.350	0.200	0.300	0.650	0.250	0.450	0.400	0.300	0.250
	Recall	**0.180**	0.090	0.090	0.030	0.070	0.040	0.060	0.130	0.050	0.090	0.080	0.060	0.050
	F-score	**0.300**	0.150	0.150	0.050	0.117	0.067	0.100	0.217	0.083	0.150	0.133	0.100	0.083
Tiger	Precision	0.800	0.450	0.500	0.450	0.500	0.450	0.500	**0.800**	0.100	0.750	0.750	0.350	0.550
	Recall	0.160	0.090	0.100	0.090	0.100	0.090	0.100	**0.160**	0.020	0.150	0.150	0.070	0.110
	F-score	0.267	0.150	0.167	0.150	0.167	0.150	0.167	**0.267**	0.033	0.250	0.250	0.117	0.183
River	Precision	0.900	0.650	0.700	0.650	0.700	0.550	0.550	**0.900**	0.350	0.850	0.850	0.350	0.650
	Recall	0.180	0.130	0.140	0.130	0.140	0.110	0.110	**0.180**	0.070	0.170	0.170	0.070	0.130
	F-score	0.300	0.217	0.233	0.217	0.233	0.183	0.183	**0.300**	0.117	0.283	0.283	0.117	0.217
Swimmer	Precision	0.800	**0.950**	0.950	0.900	0.950	0.850	0.900	0.900	0.600	0.800	0.800	0.700	0.750
	Recall	0.160	**0.190**	0.190	0.180	0.190	0.170	0.180	0.180	0.120	0.160	0.160	0.140	0.150
	F-score	0.267	**0.317**	0.317	0.300	0.317	0.283	0.300	0.300	0.200	0.267	0.267	0.233	0.250

Continued on next page

Table 5.6 – (Continued)

Class	Evaluation	M1	M2	M3	M4	M5	M6	M7	M8	M9	M10	M11	M12	M13
Pyramid	Precision	0.900	0.600	0.600	0.500	0.600	0.400	0.400	0.900	0.700	**0.950**	0.600	0.500	0.600
	Recall	0.180	0.120	0.120	0.100	0.120	0.080	0.080	0.180	0.140	**0.190**	0.120	0.100	0.120
	F-score	0.300	0.200	0.200	0.167	0.200	0.133	0.133	0.300	0.233	**0.317**	0.200	0.167	0.200
Vegetable	Precision	0.900	0.550	0.500	0.350	0.650	0.600	0.600	**0.900**	0.150	0.900	0.900	0.250	0.400
	Recall	0.180	0.110	0.100	0.070	0.130	0.120	0.120	**0.180**	0.030	0.180	0.180	0.050	0.080
	F-score	0.300	0.183	0.167	0.117	0.217	0.200	0.200	**0.300**	0.050	0.300	0.300	0.083	0.133
Models	Precision	0.500	0.450	0.450	0.150	0.350	0.200	0.300	**0.650**	0.250	0.450	0.400	0.300	0.250
	Recall	0.100	0.090	0.090	0.030	0.070	0.040	0.060	**0.130**	0.050	0.090	0.080	0.060	0.050
	F-score	0.167	0.150	0.150	0.050	0.117	0.067	0.100	**0.217**	0.083	0.150	0.133	0.100	0.083
Dog	Precision	0.850	0.450	0.750	0.600	0.650	0.350	0.150	**0.850**	0.400	0.800	0.650	0.100	0.550
	Recall	0.170	0.090	0.150	0.120	0.130	0.070	0.030	**0.170**	0.080	0.160	0.130	0.020	0.110
	F-score	0.283	0.150	0.250	0.200	0.217	0.117	0.050	**0.283**	0.133	0.267	0.217	0.033	0.183
Cloud	Precision	0.900	0.600	0.900	0.300	0.750	0.350	0.400	**0.950**	0.750	0.750	0.400	0.500	0.450
	Recall	0.180	0.120	0.180	0.060	0.150	0.070	0.080	**0.190**	0.150	0.150	0.080	0.100	0.090
	F-score	0.300	0.200	0.300	0.100	0.250	0.117	0.133	**0.317**	0.250	0.250	0.133	0.167	0.150
Mashroom	Precision	0.600	0.950	0.800	0.400	0.700	0.450	0.500	**0.950**	0.500	0.600	0.600	0.300	0.700
	Recall	0.120	0.190	0.160	0.080	0.140	0.090	0.100	**0.190**	0.100	0.120	0.120	0.060	0.140
	F-score	0.200	0.317	0.267	0.133	0.233	0.150	0.167	**0.317**	0.167	0.200	0.200	0.100	0.233
Monument	Precision	0.700	0.800	0.750	0.450	0.550	0.400	0.500	**0.900**	0.600	0.650	0.700	0.350	0.400
	Recall	0.140	0.160	0.150	0.090	0.110	0.080	0.100	**0.180**	0.120	0.130	0.140	0.070	0.080
	F-score	0.233	0.267	0.250	0.150	0.183	0.133	0.167	**0.300**	0.200	0.217	0.233	0.117	0.133
Art work	Precision	**1.000**	0.950	0.950	0.950	0.950	1.000	1.000	0.950	0.850	1.000	1.000	0.950	1.000
	Recall	**0.200**	0.190	0.190	0.190	0.190	0.200	0.200	0.190	0.170	0.200	0.200	0.190	0.200
	F-score	**0.333**	0.317	0.317	0.317	0.317	0.333	0.333	0.317	0.283	0.333	0.333	0.317	0.333
African	Precision	0.900	0.900	0.850	0.750	0.850	0.800	0.900	**0.950**	0.500	0.900	0.900	0.550	0.950
	Recall	0.180	0.180	0.170	0.150	0.170	0.160	0.180	**0.190**	0.100	0.180	0.180	0.110	0.190

Continued on next page

Table 5.6 – (Continued)

Class	Evaluation	M1	M2	M3	M4	M5	M6	M7	M8	M9	M10	M11	M12	M13
	F-score	0.300	0.300	0.283	0.250	0.283	0.267	0.300	**0.317**	0.167	0.300	0.300	0.183	0.317
Glass	Precision	0.950	0.800	0.750	0.850	0.800	0.800	0.500	0.950	0.600	**1.000**	1.000	0.650	0.900
	Recall	0.190	0.160	0.150	0.170	0.160	0.160	0.100	0.190	0.120	**0.200**	0.200	0.130	0.180
	F-score	0.317	0.267	0.250	0.283	0.267	0.267	0.167	0.317	0.200	**0.333**	0.333	0.217	0.300
Karate	Precision	0.950	0.950	0.950	0.800	0.950	0.850	0.900	**0.950**	0.950	0.950	0.950	0.950	0.950
	Recall	0.190	0.190	0.190	0.160	0.190	0.170	0.180	**0.190**	0.190	0.190	0.190	0.190	0.190
	F-score	0.317	0.317	0.317	0.267	0.317	0.283	0.300	**0.317**	0.317	0.317	0.317	0.317	0.317
Moon	Precision	0.350	0.450	0.300	0.450	0.250	0.600	**0.850**	0.450	0.400	0.300	0.350	0.650	0.400
	Recall	0.070	0.090	0.060	0.090	0.050	0.120	**0.170**	0.090	0.080	0.060	0.070	0.130	0.080
	F-score	0.117	0.150	0.100	0.150	0.083	0.200	**0.283**	0.150	0.133	0.100	0.117	0.217	0.133
Average	Precision	0.805	0.688	0.703	0.580	0.685	0.595	0.608	**0.853**	0.530	0.783	0.713	0.495	0.643
	Recall	0.161	0.138	0.141	0.116	0.137	0.119	0.122	**0.171**	0.106	0.157	0.143	0.099	0.129
	F-score	0.268	0.229	0.234	0.193	0.228	0.198	0.203	**0.284**	0.177	0.261	0.238	0.165	0.214

Table 5.7: Performance of FiCBIR approach with other variants on Oliva dataset in terms of precision, recall and f-score.

Class	Evaluation	M1	M2	M3	M4	M5	M6	M7	M8	M9	M10	M11	M12	M13
Open country	Precision	0.950	0.950	0.950	0.900	0.900	0.900	0.950	**1.000**	1.000	1.000	0.700	0.950	0.700
	Recall	0.046	0.046	0.046	0.044	0.044	0.044	0.046	**0.049**	0.049	0.049	0.034	0.046	0.034
	F-score	0.088	0.088	0.088	0.084	0.084	0.084	0.088	**0.093**	0.093	0.093	0.065	0.088	0.065
Coast Beaches	Precision	0.750	0.450	0.450	0.500	0.550	0.400	0.400	**0.900**	0.250	0.800	0.650	0.200	0.650
	Recall	0.042	0.025	0.025	0.028	0.031	0.022	0.022	**0.050**	0.014	0.044	0.036	0.011	0.036
	F-score	0.079	0.047	0.047	0.053	0.058	0.042	0.042	**0.095**	0.026	0.084	0.068	0.021	0.068
Forest	Precision	1.000	0.800	1.000	0.950	0.950	0.850	0.800	**1.000**	0.650	1.000	1.000	0.750	0.850
	Recall	0.061	0.049	0.061	0.058	0.058	0.052	0.049	**0.061**	0.040	0.061	0.061	0.046	0.052
	F-score	0.115	0.092	0.115	0.109	0.109	0.098	0.092	**0.115**	0.075	0.115	0.115	0.086	0.098
Highway	Precision	1.000	0.850	1.000	0.750	1.000	0.650	0.800	**1.000**	0.550	1.000	0.900	0.700	0.550
	Recall	0.077	0.065	0.077	0.058	0.077	0.050	0.062	**0.077**	0.042	0.077	0.069	0.054	0.042
	F-score	0.143	0.121	0.143	0.107	0.143	0.093	0.114	**0.143**	0.079	0.143	0.129	0.100	0.079
Intercity	Precision	0.850	0.700	0.750	0.850	0.750	0.850	0.650	**0.850**	0.350	0.850	0.850	0.600	0.750
	Recall	0.055	0.045	0.049	0.055	0.049	0.055	0.042	**0.055**	0.023	0.055	0.055	0.039	0.049
	F-score	0.104	0.085	0.091	0.104	0.091	0.104	0.079	**0.104**	0.043	0.104	0.104	0.073	0.091
Mountains	Precision	0.900	0.850	0.950	0.600	0.600	0.350	0.400	**1.000**	0.400	0.750	0.600	0.350	0.500
	Recall	0.048	0.045	0.051	0.032	0.032	0.019	0.021	**0.053**	0.021	0.040	0.032	0.019	0.027
	F-score	0.091	0.086	0.096	0.061	0.061	0.036	0.041	**0.102**	0.041	0.076	0.061	0.036	0.051
Streets	Precision	0.950	0.900	0.950	0.750	0.800	0.850	0.900	**0.950**	0.500	0.950	0.900	0.900	0.900
	Recall	0.065	0.062	0.065	0.051	0.055	0.058	0.062	**0.065**	0.034	0.065	0.062	0.062	0.062
	F-score	0.122	0.115	0.122	0.096	0.103	0.109	0.115	**0.122**	0.064	0.122	0.115	0.115	0.115
Tall Buildings	Precision	0.950	0.750	0.850	0.700	0.750	0.550	0.500	**1.000**	0.650	0.950	0.850	0.550	0.450
	Recall	0.053	0.042	0.048	0.039	0.042	0.031	0.028	**0.056**	0.037	0.053	0.048	0.031	0.025
	F-score	0.101	0.080	0.090	0.074	0.080	0.059	0.053	**0.106**	0.069	0.101	0.090	0.059	0.048

Continued on next page

Table 5.7 – (Continued)

Class	Evaluation	M1	M2	M3	M4	M5	M6	M7	M8	M9	M10	M11	M12	M13
Average	Precision	0.919	0.781	0.863	0.750	0.788	0.675	0.675	**0.963**	0.544	0.913	0.806	0.625	0.669
	Recall	0.055	0.047	0.051	0.045	0.047	0.040	0.040	**0.057**	0.032	0.054	0.048	0.037	0.040
	F-score	0.103	0.088	0.097	0.084	0.088	0.076	0.076	**0.108**	0.061	0.103	0.091	0.070	0.075

Table 5.4 shows the retrieval performance of thirteen CBIR methods on Wang dataset [155]. It can be observed from Table 5.4 that the proposed method (**M8**) gives better performance for all categories of images in Wang dataset with an average precision of 93.5%, recall of 18.7% and f-score of 31.2%.

Similarly, Table 5.5 shows the results of GHIM-10k [156] dataset. The proposed approach outperforms in 17 out of 20 categories and the average precision, recall and f-score are 86.5%, 3.5% and 6.7%, respectively.

To test the robustness of the **M8** method, the experiments were conducted on COREL-10k [157] dataset. The retrieved results are shown in Table 5.6. From Table 5.6, it is observed that the **M8** method provides better results in 12 out of 20 categories of images with average precision of 85.3%, recall of 17.1% and f-score of 28.4%.

Finally, the retrieval performance of all 13 CBIR variants (**M1 to M13**) are tested on Oliva [158] dataset. The **M8** method outperforms in all eight categories of images and gives the average precision, recall and f-score of 96.3%, 5.7% and 10.8%, respectively.

Table 5.8: Performance of FiCBIR approach on Wang dataset with other state-of-the-art approaches.

Class	Evaluation	(a)	(b)	(c)	(d)	(e)	(f)	(g)	(h)
Africa	Precision	0.703	0.683	0.720	0.453	0.424	0.748	0.950	**0.950**
	Recall	0.141	0.137	0.144	0.091	0.085	0.150	0.190	**0.190**
	Fscore	0.234	0.228	0.240	0.151	0.141	0.249	0.317	**0.317**
Beach	Precision	0.561	0.540	0.400	0.398	0.446	0.582	0.600	**0.800**
	Recall	0.112	0.108	0.080	0.080	0.089	0.116	0.200	**0.160**
	Fscore	0.187	0.180	0.133	0.133	0.149	0.194	0.20	**0.267**
Building	Precision	0.571	0.562	0.600	0.374	0.411	0.621	0.550	**0.950**
	Recall	0.114	0.112	0.120	0.075	0.082	0.124	0.110	**0.190**
	Fscore	0.190	0.187	0.200	0.125	0.137	0.207	0.183	**0.317**
Bus	Precision	0.876	0.888	0.500	0.741	0.852	0.802	1.000	**1.000**
	Recall	0.175	0.178	0.100	0.148	0.170	0.160	0.200	**0.200**
	Fscore	0.292	0.296	0.167	0.247	0.284	0.267	0.333	**0.333**
Dinosaur	Precision	0.987	0.992	0.950	0.915	0.587	1.000	1.000	**1.000**
	Recall	0.197	0.198	0.190	0.183	0.117	0.200	0.200	**0.200**
	Fscore	0.329	0.331	0.317	0.305	0.196	0.333	0.333	**0.333**
Elephant	Precision	0.675	0.658	0.600	0.304	0.426	0.751	0.900	**0.900**
	Recall	0.135	0.132	0.120	0.061	0.085	0.150	0.180	**0.180**
	Fscore	0.225	0.219	0.200	0.101	0.142	0.250	0.300	**0.300**
Flower	Precision	0.914	0.891	0.800	0.852	0.898	0.923	1.000	**1.000**
	Recall	0.183	0.178	0.160	0.170	0.180	0.185	0.200	**0.200**
	Fscore	0.305	0.297	0.267	0.284	0.299	0.308	0.333	**0.333**
Horse	Precision	0.834	0.803	0.630	0.568	0.589	0.896	1.000	**1.000**
	Recall	0.167	0.161	0.126	0.114	0.118	0.179	0.200	**0.200**
	Fscore	0.278	0.268	0.210	0.189	0.196	0.299	0.333	**0.333**
Mountain	Precision	0.536	0.522	0.300	0.293	0.268	0.561	0.750	**0.750**
	Recall	0.107	0.104	0.060	0.059	0.054	0.112	0.150	**0.150**
	Fscore	0.179	0.174	0.100	0.098	0.089	0.187	0.250	**0.250**
Food	Precision	0.741	0.733	0.400	0.369	0.427	0.803	1.000	**1.000**
	Recall	0.148	0.147	0.080	0.074	0.085	0.161	0.200	**0.200**
	Fscore	0.247	0.244	0.133	0.123	0.142	0.268	0.333	**0.333**
Average	Precision	0.739	0.727	0.590	0.527	0.533	0.769	0.875	**0.935**
	Recall	0.148	0.145	0.118	0.105	0.107	0.154	0.175	**0.187**
	Fscore	0.246	0.242	0.197	0.176	0.178	0.256	0.292	**0.312**

Techniques: (a)- ElAlami [161] (b)- Lin et al. [165] (c)- Wang et al. [82] (d)- Jhanwar et al. [166] (e)- Huang and Dai [167] (f)- Shrivastava and Tyagi [134] (g)- Pradhan et al. [94] (h)- FiCBIR (Proposed)

From the experimental results presented in Tables 5.4 to 5.7, it has been noticed that

Chapter 5 Implementation Details and Experimental Results

the method **M8** consistently provides better results for all four datasets as compared to other variants. Further, to validate the efficacy of **M8** (the proposed approach), it has been compared with seven other related CBIR systems: Elalami *et al.* [161], Chuen *et al.* [165], Wang *et al.* [82], Jhanwar *et al.* [166], Huang and Dai *et al.* [167], Shrivastava and Tyagi [134], and Pradhan *et al.* [94] on Wang dataset.

Table 5.8 shows the comparative results of the proposed approach along with seven other related CBIR approaches on Wang dataset. It has been observed that the proposed approach gives the average precision of 93.5%, recall of 18.7% and f-score of 31.2% which is better than the other state-of-the-art approaches (Table 5.8) .

Further, the results are also illustrated graphically, Fig. 5.8(a), Fig. 5.8(b) and Fig. 5.8(c) show the precision, recall and f-score, respectively. From the Fig. 5.8(a), Fig. 5.8(b) and Fig. 5.8(c) it is observed that the proposed CBIR approach (**M8**) is better than the other state-of-the-art CBIR approaches for all categories of images.

5.3.1 Number of Processing Steps and Retrieval Precision in FiCBIR

In this section, number of processing step required for single layer (**M1**), three layers (**M2**) and proposed (**M8**) CBIR approach are discussed. Let F_1, F_2 and F_3 be the color, texture and shape feature vectors, respectively. The size of feature vectors F_1, F_2 and F_3 are 81, 60 and 21, respectively.

$$F_1 \approx \frac{4}{3} \times F_2 \tag{5.17}$$

$$F_1 \approx 4 \times F_3 \tag{5.18}$$

$$F_2 \approx 3 \times F_3 \tag{5.19}$$

From the length of feature vectors, Eq. (5.17), Eq. (5.18) and Eq. (5.19) are derived. Let image dataset contains N images. Approach **M1** (Table 4.5) uses three features and combines them to form a single feature vector for each image. On similar lines, query image is also converted into feature vector. The search process computes similarity

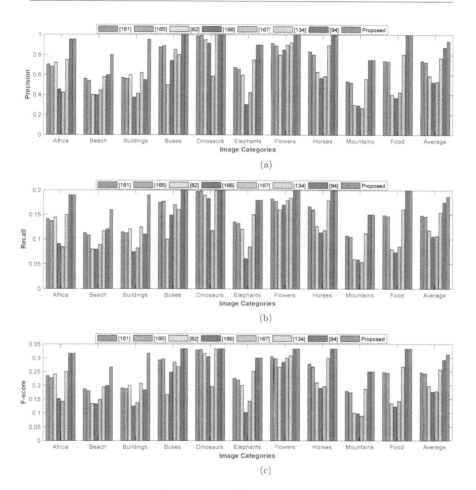

Figure 5.8: Precision: 5.8(a), recall: 5.8(b) and f-score 5.8(c) of FiCBIR and existing CBIR approaches for Wang dataset

between query image and dataset images based on feature vector content and 20 most similar images are retrieved. Total Processing Steps (TPS) required are:

$$TPS = N \times [|F_1| + |F_2| + |F_3|] \qquad (5.20)$$

Chapter 5 Implementation Details and Experimental Results   105

By substituting F_1 and F_2 with F_3 from Eq. (5.18) and Eq. (5.19) and we get Eq. (5.21).

$TPS \approx N \times [4 \times |F_3| + 3 \times |F_3| + |F_3|]$

$$TPS \approx 8 \times N \times F_3 \qquad (5.21)$$

CBIR approaches, **M2** and **M8**, use layer-wise image retrieval. In layer L_1 all images are compared with query image, layer L_2 compares only 10% of total (N) images whereas layer L_3 compares only 50% of the images compared at layer L_2.

Approach **M2** (Table 4.5) uses three layers for image retrieval, Layer L_1 uses feature F_1, Layer L_2 uses feature F_2 and the third Layer L_3 uses feature F_3.

$$TPS = N \times |F_1| + \frac{N}{10} \times |F_2| + \frac{N}{20} \times F_3 \qquad (5.22)$$

By substituting F_1 and F_2 with F_3 from Eq. (5.18) and Eq. (5.19), we get Eq. (5.23)

$$TPS \approx N \times 4 \times |F_3| + \frac{N}{10} \times 3 \times |F_3| + \frac{N}{20} \times |F_3| N \times 4 \times |F_3| + \frac{N}{10} \times 3 \times |F_3| + \frac{N}{20} \times |F_3| \qquad (5.23)$$

$$TPS \approx \frac{87 \times N \times |F_3|}{20} \qquad (5.24)$$

$$TPS \approx 4.35 \times N \times |F_3| \qquad (5.25)$$

From the Eq. 5.21 and Eq. 5.25 it is observed that **M2** takes less than half number of processing steps as compared to **M1**.

The total processing steps for proposed approach, *i.e.*, **M8** (Table 4.5) are:

$$TPS = N \times |F_1| + \frac{N}{10} \times [|F_1| + |F_2|] + \frac{N}{20} \times [|F_1| + |F_2| + |F_3|] \qquad (5.26)$$

By substituting F_1 and F_2 with F_3 from Eq. (5.18) and Eq. (5.19), we get Eq. (5.27)

$$TPS \approx N \times 4 \times |F_3| + \frac{N}{10} \times [4 \times |F_3| + 3 \times |F_3|] + \frac{N}{20} \times [4 \times |F_3| + 3 \times |F_3| + |F_3|] \qquad (5.27)$$

$$TPS \approx \frac{102 \times N \times F_3}{20} \qquad (5.28)$$

$$TPS \approx 5.1 \times N \times F_3 \qquad (5.29)$$

It is observed from the Eq. 5.29 and Eq. 5.25 that **M8** takes slightly more number of processing steps as compared to **M2** but this computation cost provides almost 17% higher average precision in the retrieval process.

Space complexity of FiCBIR: FiCBIR uses three layers for image retrieval and three types of image feature, at first layer it uses one image feature, say F_1, at second layer F_1 and F_2 features are considered and at layer three, all three features, F_1, F_2 and F_3 are considered.

Case I: Memory required to store database consisting of features extracted from N images (for similarity computation) is $N \times (|F_1| + |F_2| + |F_3|)$

Case II: Memory required in layered approach:

L_1: $N \times max(|F_1|, |F_2|, |F_3|)$ (All feature combinations are considered)

L_2: $(N/10) \times max((|F_1| + |F_2|), (|F_1| + |F_3|), (|F_2| + |F_3|))$

L_3: $(N/20) \times (|F_1| + |F_2| + |F_3|)$

Among the all three layers, L_1, L_2 and L_3; L_1 takes maximum space thus space used by L_1 is considered for comparison.

Memory required in Case II is $N \times max(|F_1|, |F_2|, |F_3|)$ which is always less than that required in Case I.

Chapter 6 concludes the entire thesis and provide the major contributions along with future directions for this research work.

Chapter 6

Conclusion and Future Scope

In this work three similarity search approaches have been designed. First similarity search approach is proposed for textual dataset, it uses GPU to support parallel computing. Second and third approaches are proposed for image datasets which use CBIR approaches where more than one layers are considered for retrieval process and images are represented using color, texture and shape features.

6.1 Conclusion

PCASSB, a parallel similarity search approach for text documents uses Bloom filter and integer array for representing the documents and query features, respectively. In this approach, shingles are used to represent the features of documents and query. Further, these feature sets are mapped to Bloom filters for quick similarity computation. The proposed approach exploit the GPU computability for processing text documents for similarity search. Effectiveness of the proposed approach has been tested on 20Newsgroup dataset. The proposed work has been tested on single GPU and it is quite efficient in performing parallel similarity search.

Further for image datasets two CBIR approaches have been proposed; First CBIR approach (BiCBIR) uses color, texture and shape features to represent query and dataset images. The retrieval module of the proposed approach consists of two layers; in the first layer, it compares texture and shape features and most relevant images are passed to the next layer. In the second layer, color and shape features are matched and the most similar images are returned to the user in response to the query image. Based on the experimental analysis, the best feature sequence has been selected for image retrieval. The retrieval results show that the precision is high when texture and shape features are considered for the first layer while shape and color features are considered for the second layer. Experimental results indicate that the proposed approach is accurate and faster in terms of time requirement.

Second CBIR approach named as 'Efficient layer-wise feature incremental approach for CBIR system' has been proposed which uses three image features for comparing visual similarity between query and dataset images. It has been tested on four image datasets. The performance of the proposed approach has been evaluated on the basis of precision, recall and f-score. The experimental results validate that the performance of CBIR system enhances when layer-wise feature incremental approach is implemented.

6.2 Contributions

In this work three similarity search approaches have been proposed and the major contributions are:

- PCASSB uses GPU for parallel processing and Bloom filters to represent the documents in compressed form. Bloom filters support parallelism which require very less computation, thus suits well with GPU.

- BiCBIR uses three image features and two layers for retrieval process. In this approach, total number of comparisons are reduced while maintaining the accuracy. The core idea of the proposed approach is to use a common image feature in both the layer which contributes the similarity in the second layer, computed at the first layer. It also reduces the search space for the second layer since only relevant images are compared.

- Third approach (FiCBIR) uses three image features and three retrieval layers. In this approach image features are added at every layer and dataset size is reduced in subsequent layers. This feature incremental approach helps to preserve the similarity computed at previous layer for the next layer. The three retrieval layers used in the proposed approach helps to reduce the number of comparisons.

- The proposed approaches can be utilized in the following ways: PCASSB can be used for plagiarism detection, information retrieval and recommender system where textual datasets are used. BiCBIR and FiCBIR proposed CBIR approaches are useful where image datasets are involved like searching on e-commerce websites using product image, identity verification, *etc.*

6.3 Future Scope

The main focus in this work is on similarity search but some other factors also show high impact on similarity search such as type of features, feature merging and ordering to represent the items efficiently. Future directions can be:

- PCASSB is designed for textual dataset which uses single GPU. Parallelism exploited using single GPU can be extended for multiple GPUs which will further accelerate the similarity search process. With multiple GPUs, the proposed approach can be used for bigger datasets. Further, Bloom filter with less collisions and less false positive rate can also be considered to increase the accuracy of the proposed approach to some extend.

- Second and third approaches are used for image dataset, and uses color, texture and shape features. These features can be merged with some advanced fusion technique which can help to improve the accuracy of the proposed work. In this work, multiple retrieval layers are fixed. To further enhance the performance of the approaches based upon the application's requirement, the number of layers can be reconfigured dynamically to accelerate the retrieval process. Further, parallelism can also be incorporated in these two CBIR approaches to speed-up the retrieval process.

- Indexing or partitioning of image datasets based on the subset of feature space may speed-up the process as clustering may be helpful to reduce the search time.

CPSIA information can be obtained
at www.ICGtesting.com
Printed in the USA
BVHW062201170223
658733BV00018B/1780